Rita,

Thinking of you
this Holiday Season!

Stephen K.

D0049045

One
Simple
Idea

Turn Your Dreams into a LICENSING GOLDMINE While Letting OTHERS DO THE WORK

STEPHEN KEY

New York   Chicago   San Francisco   Lisbon   London   Madrid   Mexico City
Milan   New Delhi   San Juan   Seoul   Singapore   Sydney   Toronto

The *McGraw·Hill* Companies

1 2 3 4 5 6 7 8 9 10 11 12 13 14 15   QFR/QFR   1 9 8 7 6 5 4 3 2 1

ISBN   978-0-07-175615-0
MHID   0-07-175615-9

Library of Congress Cataloging-in-Publication Data

Key, Stephen.
      One simple idea : turn your dreams into a licensing goldmine while letting others
    do the work / Stephen Key.
          p.   cm.
      ISBN 978-0-07-175615-0 (hardback)
      1. Inventions—Marketing.   2. Entrepreneurship.   3. Inventions.   4. New
    business enterprises—Management.   I. Title.

    T339.K49   2011
    658.1—dc22   2010047471

Interior design by Monica Baziuk

McGraw-Hill books are available at special quantity discounts to use as premiums and sales promotions or for use in corporate training programs. To contact a representative, please e-mail us at bulksales@mcgraw-hill.com.

This book is printed on acid-free paper.

To Janice, my wife, my life

Contents

Preface

The Ferriss Effect

BACK IN 2003, when I first started teaching my "10 Steps to Bring Your Idea to Market" course, a guy who didn't look much like a student started showing up at my classes. Unusually fit, he wore leather from head to toe and carried a motorcycle helmet. Long after everyone else had settled down, he would walk in and scan the room for the perfect spot to sit and focus. Thus positioned, he would cock his head and fix a penetrating look at either my partner Andrew or me as we spoke from the front of the room. I got the sense he was absorbing every story, statistic, and strategy we shared and was turning them over in his mind.

At the end of class, students would mill around deferentially, eager to ask questions. But Tim Ferriss didn't waste time on small talk.

"Let's go out for gin and tonics," he proposed. "I need to know more."

I waved him off at first, but he persisted. He wanted to learn how I had become my own boss with tens of thousands of people, whom I didn't know, working for me. Eventually, I went out for those drinks, in part just to shut him up. Tim has got to be the most persistent individual I've ever met, and he drilled me about what I do and how he could apply my experiences to his business. You see, Tim had created a dietary supplement, Brain Quicken, and like many entrepreneurs, he had also launched a company to manufacture and market it. Now he wanted to do what I do: get a licensee to manufacture and market his idea *for* him so he could kick back and collect royalty checks.

Eventually, Tim took off to travel the world, calling in periodically for more advice about how to turn his company from a time-sucking machine into a passive-income generator. One day in 2005, he called me from Argentina, where he was studying tango, to announce he was writing a book. He asked me to read what he had written thus far.

Tim's book came to be titled *The 4-Hour Workweek*, and it quickly climbed to the number one spot on the *New York Times* bestseller list. The lessons Tim learned from my classes helped him form the book's underlying philosophy. In it, he coins the term "lifestyle design" and describes me as a member of "a quiet subculture of people called the 'new rich'"—people who have escaped the rat race and discovered how to live the life they want to.

My teaching had begun as a sideline to my product development work, but a few months after Tim's book came out, a flood of new students began signing up for our course. "Wow," I said to my wife one day after I got home, "We're going to have to start taking this seriously."

Thanks to what I now call "the Ferriss effect," the number of my students keeps growing. I have now taught people from more than 30 countries, including Australia, Bolivia, Costa Rica, Chile, Norway, Iceland, Singapore, and Canada. The strategies I teach can work for anyone anywhere.

My students hunger to pick up where *The 4-Hour Workweek* leaves off, which is what my classes and this book do. For the last 30 years, I've designed my lifestyle by "renting" my ideas out to large corporations. What I do and how I do it is simple, even if it isn't always easy. However, it is easier today than it has ever been before because of a phenomenon called "open innovation," which anyone at all—regardless of education or background—can take advantage of.

One of my life's passions is teaching others my roadmap for jumping into the innovation stream and becoming their own boss. I've condensed my teachings into the nineteen easy-to-read chapters in this book. Whether people learn this road map from me or figure it out for themselves, I believe many, many more people will begin designing their lifestyles this way in the future.

Although Tim came to me for help at first, he ended up returning the favor.

Tim, next time you're in town, drinks are on me.

Acknowledgments

First and foremost, I want to thank my wife, Janice, for allowing me to pursue my dreams. I don't think there is any greater gift one can give. I know it hasn't always been easy living with Peter Pan, yet you continue to be the most remarkable, smart, and beautiful woman I have ever met. I want to thank my children, who also have had to put up with me over the years. Your dad has never had a traditional job, but you've all been patient with me throughout the ups and downs. I am so proud of each of you and what you have accomplished.

James Shehan, you make me look so good. You've been an incredibly loyal assistant and friend. I thank you for that. I don't know anyone who possesses all of the skills and talent that you do. I'm constantly impressed by your genius. And you put up with me too—which may be the most challenging task of all! I look forward to the next ten years.

I need to thank my business partner, Andrew Krauss, for helping me start this journey. I have never met anyone who is so giving of himself. Your dedication to the inventing community is remarkable. I appreciate everything you do.

Linda Pollock, I want to thank you for being my absolute first student and believing in me and supporting me all these years. You have become a true friend.

My mentor, Stephen Askin, has been incredibly supportive of me as well. You gave me my first opportunity to succeed when I was just beginning my career—everyone else thought I was crazy, but you believed in me! Your guidance and encouragement gave me the confidence I needed. I have watched you continue to mentor other individuals with all your heart and soul. Thank you.

Tim Ferriss, you helped spread my message across the world as you spread your own. I can't thank you enough for this.

My literary agent, Kirsten Neuhaus—thank you for teaching me how to write a book and for holding my hand throughout the journey.

I want to thank my editor, Gary Krebs, for understanding my vision and for helping me focus my material. You are truly great at what you do.

Colleen Sell, you are more than a collaborator. You went beyond the call of duty in helping produce this book. You understood the content as well as my voice. Thank you for being such an integral part of our team.

John Kimball, my father-in-law, you've been tough on me over the years, but through it all you have been my biggest supporter. You are my second father. I've enjoyed our Friday evening talks more than you will ever know. Thank you for your wisdom.

And finally, I would like to thank my father. The business principles you instilled in me are the ones I continue to live by and to share with my students. These are the principles that have made me the man I am today. I've followed my passion, Dad. Life *is* too short, and I've been enjoying it all I can.

Introduction

How One Simple Idea Led to
the Life of My Dreams

Hi, my name is Stephen Key, and I am a successful entrepreneur and licensing expert. I don't have a degree in engineering, marketing, or business. I don't own a big company, nor am I employed by a big company. Instead, companies work for me—bringing my product ideas to life while I sit back collecting royalty checks, creating new product ideas, and enjoying the life of my dreams with my beautiful wife and our three children. And I wrote this book to show you how you can do the same thing and reap the same kind of benefits.

But before I tell you how to bring your ideas to life, let me tell you a little more about me . . . because I have a feeling we're a lot alike. From an early age, I dreamed of being an entrepreneur. But I didn't want to go to college for four or six or more years to study how to create and manage a business. I didn't want to run a business with a lot of employees, overhead, debt, hassles, and headaches. I didn't want to live to work, as so many business owners and professionals do. Instead, I wanted to work to live—and to live well. More than anything, I wanted to create stuff. Have fun! See the world! Have a family! Enjoy life!

That's exactly what I've been doing for almost 30 years. I just wish someone would have told me the secrets of the game—the secrets I'm going to tell you in this book—when I started out on this journey.

My first foray as an entrepreneur was to design sculpted plush animals and characters, which I made myself and sold at art shows and state fairs. That's when I learned my first big lesson in product design. Let's face it, when the rent is due and you're hungry, if the product you've spent several hours making doesn't sell, you quickly move on to something else.

Before long, representatives from toy companies began to notice my creations, and I started designing products for Dakin, Inc., on a freelance basis. Then I got my first "real job" —you know, the kind with a regular paycheck—at a start-up company called Worlds of Wonder (WOW). I figured I could work at WOW during the day and do my freelance projects at night, doubling my earnings. As it turned out, I spent far more time overseeing the manufacture of products than I did designing them. Still, as head of the design group at WOW, I was involved in the design (not the creation, but the manufacturing and design) of several hit toys, such as Teddy Ruxpin, the world's first talking teddy bear, and Lazer Tag, the top-selling toy of 1986. But I would often look at the new product ideas that came in and think, *I can do better than that!*

So after two years I left WOW to start my own toy creation, design, and licensing company. For a while, to pay the rent, I continued to do freelance design for toy manufacturers, including Disney, Applause, Dakin, and WOW, among others. Now I focus solely on creating and licensing my own ideas.

I've licensed more than 20 ideas for products in such diverse fields as the toy, beverage, music, novelty, and pharmaceutical industries. Celebrities Michael Jordan and Alex Trebek have served as pitchmen for two of my products. Collectively, my creations have sold more than a half billion units and generated billions of dollars of retail revenue. I have served as a consultant on the reality show "American Inventor" and been featured on the CNBC show "The Big Idea with Donny Deutsch." I am invited to speak at U.S. Patent and Trademark

Office events, Stanford University, IDEO (one of the world's top design firms), and elsewhere, and I teach my "invent right" strategies to thousands of people.

My product ideas range from the simple to the silly to the life-saving. In my view, good ideas are those that sell—plain and simple. I dreamt up a Valentine's Day dart with a suction cup and a flag reading, "I'm stuck on you." That idea brought me $10,000 in advance income with zero upfront investment. I re-envisioned the plain gray guitar pick as a blank slate for new colors and designs—paisley patterns and skull shapes, to name but a few—as well as for marketing tie-ins, such as names of bands and artists, including Taylor Swift. This simple insight upped a 25¢ purchase to a $1 purchase, and has sold 20 million picks.

One of my favorite early ideas is a small basketball backboard designed to look like a basketball player with his arms outstretched. Ohio Art licensed that idea from me and sold more than one million Michael Jordan Wall Balls the first year! One of my most successful ideas is the Spinformation rotating label, which adds 75 percent more information to bottle labels and has sold more than 400 million units worldwide. In its newest incarnation, the Spinformation label as sold by Accudial Pharmaceutical, Inc., is helping prevent the estimated 30,000 cases of medicinal over- and under-dosing of children nationally.

On any given day, I've got six new ideas out to different companies. Like my students, I'm still creating.

I've had a fantastic time creating new product ideas and "renting" them to manufacturers. It's fun. It's exciting. I'm never bored. I never run out of ideas. I never have to worry about going to work for someone else. And I never worry about money, even though I don't claim to be good with money in the conventional sense.

I have many friends who spend all their time trying to figure out how to increase their wealth. They're obsessed with investing in the market and paying less in taxes. I could not care less. Money for money's sake doesn't interest me. When the stock market crashed, I was unaffected; I wasn't in it. When the recession hit, it didn't impact me.

Two of my children attend Berkeley, and the youngest is a freshman at the University of Oregon. I will pay for all of their college educations, comfortably.

My beautiful wife and I are totally debt free. We have chosen to live in Modesto, a small California town surrounded by farms and vineyards. We moved here for my wife's job more than 20 years ago, and it's been a great place to raise kids. I, of course, can do my work anywhere. I have a small office a few miles from home. And one employee—just one.

Our home, though lovely, is a tract house in a nice but nondescript neighborhood. We own it outright. Although our home is not lavish, it is by our choice, and we do not live a "practical" lifestyle. The cars we drive, all purchased with cash, are probably too expensive. And it probably wasn't practical for us to take the kids out of school and for me not to go into the office for a month so we could go to Africa, or for six months so we could travel the United States together.

Sometimes, I still can't believe that I've been doing this for almost 30 years and making a living at it—a good living. It wasn't easy at first. It has taken a lot of hard work, and I've learned a lot along the way. I have made a lot of money and lost some as well. But I've had a ball.

Anybody can do what I've done, including you. I don't have a background in sales or marketing or engineering. All I have are ideas. Some of my ideas are great; some are OK; some are lousy. It doesn't matter whether your idea is big or small. It doesn't have to change the world. It doesn't have to be the next best thing since sliced bread. And you don't have to quit your day job to start creating and licensing ideas. All it takes is *one simple idea*—and the ability to translate it into a product that consumers want and that a company will want to make and market for you.

I've been doing this for many years, and I've taught thousands of other people how to "invent right" too. Now with this book, I'm sharing this amazingly simple strategy with you, so that you, too, can live the life of your dreams by creating great product ideas and licensing them to companies.

"If you can dream it, you can do it."

—Walt Disney

PART ONE

The Power of One Simple Idea

How would you like to wake up every day eager to go to work? Better yet, how would you like to work for yourself—focusing on what you want and love to do? Even better yet, how would you like for your entrepreneurial enterprise to give you the time, energy, money, and freedom to live the life of your dreams?

All you need is one simple idea . . . and a simple strategy for bringing your ideas to market.

How You Can Create the Life of Your Dreams

ARE YOU a creative type who is always envisioning new and better ways to do things? Do you constantly think of ways to make things more efficient or enjoyable, more aesthetically pleasing, or just plain more fun? Do you often see ways to improve or enhance the products and services you use regularly, or ways to give them more pizzazz? Have you ever wished that *you* could be the one to bring those ideas to life . . . and actually make a living doing it?

Or are you one of the millions of people world-wide who are unemployed? Do you want a livelihood that can't be snatched away tomorrow through a single stroke of bad luck, like a layoff or illness? Or are you one of the many millions more who are underemployed, struggling to make ends meet and bored to tears in a dead-end job? Do you need to find a way to supplement your day job without running yourself ragged? Do you dream of having a job that doesn't squander your talents and limit your earning potential?

Or perhaps you're like me. You know life is short, and you don't want to waste it working just to pay bills and to build up your retirement account. You want to work in an industry that interests you, to do work you're passionate about, to have the means and the freedom to pursue your personal interests, to spend quality time with family and friends, to travel—to enjoy life.

That's what I wanted. And that's exactly what I've been doing—dreaming up ideas, licensing them to companies, and living the life of my dreams. That's right. I *rent* my ideas to other companies. While they're making and marketing the stuff I've dreamed up, I'm collecting the rent for those ideas and doing what I love to do: create.

Every day, tens of thousands of people all over the world are working for me: box boys, cashiers, truck drivers, printers, fabricators, accountants, marketing execs, sales reps, researchers, human resource administrators, and presidents and CEOs of companies like Ohio Art, Nestle, Jim Beam, Toys "R" Us, Walgreens, Walmart, and others all are laboring on my behalf. They take care of the research and development, production, marketing and sales, customer service, accounting, and everything else that goes into producing and selling my creations . . . so I don't have to. My creativity fuels their production, and I leverage their immense power. I have found a way to make the system work for me rather than the other way around.

You can, too. All it takes is one simple idea—one that's ripe for the marketplace.

The reason I can do this—and the reason you and anyone else can too—is because of a trend called "open innovation" that is reshaping the business world. In the past, most new product and service ideas came from inside a company or from a big design firm. Rarely would these big corporations even consider ideas from an "outsider" like me—a regular guy with no credentials in engineering, marketing, or design, but with a creative bent and a penchant for dreaming up cool stuff. Now for the first time in history, companies are realizing that maybe, just maybe, they don't have all the world's smartest and most creative people working in their companies. They have finally grasped that they can, and must, find new and innovative ideas from the outside.

You can find many academic books on the subject of open innovation, but this is the first book to explain why open innovation is important to you and how you can use it to become a successful entrepreneur—as you'll learn in Chapter 2. Today, companies need help. They need people like you and me. It doesn't matter if you're a stay-at-home mom, a truck driver, an aerospace engineer, or a teacher. It doesn't matter whether you have a Ph.D. or are a high school dropout. To play the biggest, most exciting game in the world—coming up with new, or improved, or jazzed-up products and services—your credentials are irrelevant. All you need is a simple idea and a simple strategy for bringing that idea to market.

Is It Really That Simple?

Oh, here they come . . . all those "but" questions buzzing around in your brain. I knew they would, and I understand. What I just said and what I'm about to tell you flies in the face of conventional wisdom. Later, I'll explain how my strategy turns conventional wisdom on its head and traditional methods of innovation into the dinosaurs they are. First, though, let's get those nay-saying questions out of the way.

But Don't I Need to Start a Company?

You no longer have to start a company to experience the entrepreneurial thrill of innovating. As you'll learn in Chapter 3, licensing your ideas lets you focus on the most exciting part of any business and leave the tough stuff, like manufacturing, marketing, and distribution, to others.

With the global recession and the wars that are weighing our country down, you hear a lot of doomsayers forecasting the end of the American Dream. My students and I—and many others I have never met—provide living proof that the American Dream has far from expired. In fact, it is more alive, more accessible, and far more exciting today than it ever has been in the history of our country. You'll read many of our stories and learn all about this exciting new world of innovation and how to be a part of it throughout this book.

But Do I Need to Quit My Day Job?

Absolutely not. In fact, I recommend that you do *not* quit your day job—until and unless you have the passion to create and license ideas as a profession, *and* have a few successes under your belt, *and* have sufficient royalties coming into your bank account. As I always tell my inventRight students, licensing is a numbers game. Most people have to come up with a lot of ideas before one gets licensed. It can also take time to find a licensee and for the licensee to bring your idea to market.

The great thing about licensing ideas is that it doesn't have to be a 40-hour-a-week job, even for those who are ready, willing, and able to do it "full time." When you're first starting out or if you're doing this as a hobby or to supplement your day job, you can do this in as little as 10 hours a week or less using my 10-step strategy for creating and licensing ideas.

But Don't I Need a Patent?

Well no, and maybe yes. In my experience, you do not have to put your financial security at risk to innovate. You don't have to take out a mortgage on your home or empty out your retirement savings to get a patent on your idea. You do not need patents to license ideas, and product cycles churn so quickly that you will lose your opportunity if you spend the years and tens of thousands of dollars it takes to get a patent.

Besides, if you think a patent guarantees you protection, you're crazy. First-to-market owns the shelf space. That's the best protection you can have. In Chapter 11, I'll show you the smart way to play the patent game. I have more than a dozen patents myself. For now, just realize that patents are not nearly as important as you think they are. It really depends on the idea/invention. Read Chapter 11 to help you decide!

But Isn't It Really Hard to Do This?

Back when I first started licensing my ideas to big companies, it was much harder to do than it is now. Today, the pace of business is so fast and products come and go so quickly that companies simply do not have the ability to do it all on their own. Consequently, many companies have opened their doors to independent product developers like you and me—a movement called "open innovation," which you'll learn more about in Chapter 2. The 10-step process that I teach my inventRight students and that I've outlined in this book makes it easy for anyone to create and license ideas.

But What If I Don't Have Any Ideas?

Everyone has ideas. You're a consumer, right? By virtue of being a consumer, you have plenty of opinions about all the products and services you buy and use at home, at work, and at play. So you do have innovative ideas. It's those ideas that companies desperately want and need. It's those ideas that can help you go into business for yourself without having to start and run a company with a lot of overhead, equipment, and people. You just need to learn how to translate those ideas into a marketable product and how to get your ideas into the right hands and in the right way. That's what this book is all about.

But if dreaming up product ideas is truly not your thing, you can still get into the innovation game by becoming a connector—a product scout—someone who brings other people's ideas to companies who want and need them.

Whether you're a creator or connector, these ideas do not have to be mind-blowing. They don't have to change the world. No reinventing the wheel here, I tell my students. Companies can make huge gains from small, incremental changes and from slight improvements to existing products.

I've been swimming in the innovation stream for more than three decades, so I know where and how to look for ideas. In Part Two, I show you how to brainstorm ideas and pick the best ones to develop for licensing. I also tell you where and how to find products and industries in need of refreshing.

But How Do I Start?

My dad spent his entire career at General Electric. He was a project manager, and he loved his job. He never thought of himself as going to work. He was just doing what he loved. When I was struggling back in my 20s, making and selling toys at craft fairs, Dad told me, "Find what your passion is. Make it your career, and you will never 'work' a day in your life."

That's where I tell my students to start: *find your passion.* Are you interested in sports? Then look there for simple ideas—existing products you can improve upon. If your passion is gardening or pets or monkey-wrenching or parenting or music or home improvement, start there. When your work is your passion, it propels you forward. And it's fun!

Sometimes I work a lot because I love what I do. But like my dad, I never feel like I'm working. Sometimes all I do for long stretches is make sure my checks are being deposited.

I like to think I took Dad's advice to heart and went one better. Although my father loved his work, he wasn't in control of it. When he was laid off, his years of loyalty were powerless against much larger economic forces. Today, I get to love my work and know that I don't have all my eggs in one basket. They're scattered about in dozens of different baskets. Even better, there's an endless supply of eggs out there for me if I need them. You have them, too.

I love being my own boss. I love coming up with new products. I love the life that creating and licensing products has enabled me and my family to live. And I'd love to help you do the same. All it takes is one simple idea.

So start with one simple idea that you're passionate about. Then follow my 10 simple steps for bringing your idea to market.

My Introduction to a New Way of Innovating

When I was in college, I didn't have it in me to be like those ultra-driven business students. I wanted to relax and have fun and make things. In fact, after my dad gave me his piece of golden advice about finding my passion, I realized that if I could come up with good ideas and make things with my hands, I would be the richest man in the world, in every sense of the word.

I switched from business classes at Santa Clara University to art classes at San Jose State University, even though I couldn't paint or sculpt as well as my classmates. A few years later, I began making stuffed toys on my own with a sewing machine. I sold them out of a booth at fairs around the state of California. My favorite part was watching my funny creations make people smile. To the world I was looking like a pretty big loser, but I loved every minute of it. I just didn't love the fact that I needed more income to do the things I wanted to do with my life, like get married, buy a home, and raise a family.

Around this time, I had another conversation with my father. This time Dad gave me his second most important piece of advice, one that he didn't follow personally but saw his employer, General Electric, put into action. This is what he told me:

- Find something that doesn't require your presence.
- Find something that doesn't require your hands.
- Make sure it has a "multiplying effect."

At first I didn't understand what he meant. But over the ensuing couple of years, I figured it out.

Here's what happened next: I knew I needed to break out of the fair circuit, so at age 27 and with a background in art, I talked myself into my first job with a start-up toy company called Worlds of Wonder. Within a year, I found myself on the manufacturing and design team that helped bring the company's most popular toy ever to market, the original storytelling teddy bear, Teddy Ruxpin. Kids were entranced by his animated ability to talk and blink his eyes. Parents could pop a cassette player in his back, and he would rivet kids to their seats by telling them stories. In 1986 alone, Worlds of Wonder sold five million Teddy Ruxpins. For a brief while, we became the fifth largest toy company in the world. All of a sudden, my future was looking bright.

You wouldn't have known that if you'd seen me after I'd stepped off a 13-hour flight to Hong Kong. Haggard and wild-eyed with jet lag, I felt like I'd just landed on the moon. The tropical heat and humidity hit me like a ton of bricks. I stumbled into my hotel room and collapsed. The next day I traveled across the border to our factory in mainland China, which was working around the clock to fulfill the demand for our bears. My job was to make sure every one that came off the line looked beautiful. The bears meant money, and we had to keep them coming. My boss had given me a parting direction in no uncertain terms: "Never stop the production line."

Standing on that production line watching bear after bear pass me by, I kept thinking about a man named Ken Forsse. Ken created Teddy Ruxpin and licensed it to Worlds of Wonder. Everyone knew he was making millions of dollars in royalties. Those numbers pinged about in my head as I watched the workers' hands move rapidly over soft brown fabric.

Something was inspiring about this equation. The man with the idea, the one who was making lots of money, wasn't even there. We only saw him when we needed approval. He wasn't the one standing halfway across the world in a frenetic factory far from home, like me.

I finally understood what my dad was talking about and what the multiplying effect could mean. I suddenly realized I didn't want to be the guy on the line, working day in and day out. I wanted to be the other guy. Like Ken, I wanted to be the smartest guy in the room, the one collecting the checks while others were working for me. That single thought changed my life—just as so many of my ideas since then have.

When I got back to California, I decided to show my own ideas, my *own creations* for toys to our company president. He smiled and listened politely, but later my boss reprimanded me for taking my focus off our existing product lines. I knew right then I had to quit. Fortunately, by then I had years of experience as a freelance designer and a network of potential clients to fall back on. I knew WOW needed me, so I hoped they'd be my first client—and they were. I also had the support of Janice, my girlfriend and future wife, whose salary could take care of us financially until I got my feet on the ground as an independent product developer. And so with that support as my springboard, I launched Stephen Key Design, LLC, and set out to create, develop, and license my own ideas.

Flash forward to spring 2000. It's a sunny day in Boca Raton, Florida. I am standing in front of yet another production line and watching as my Spinformation label is being affixed to thousands of bottles of herbal supplements at the Rexall Sundown production facility. Watching that production line made me oddly nervous; any breakdown would mean an interruption in my income. I couldn't help but smile. Finally, I was on the right side of that upside-down equation.

This production line was printing money for me just as it had for Ken years earlier. The best part was that I didn't even have to be there. I'd only dropped by that day because I wanted to. I'd become the smartest guy in the room. By renting out ideas to others, I'd finally fulfilled my dad's prescription. I didn't have to be there for an idea to reach customers. And by getting some of the world's largest companies to work for me, I'd set in motion an awe-inspiring multiplying effect.

The crazy thing about this story is that the label itself wasn't even *my* idea. I just figured out how to manufacture it, something no one had done before. The point is: you don't even need to have your own ideas to do this.

So how did I manage to become an outsider who successfully licenses ideas? I think it's worth asking that question because part of the answer is that *I do not see problems.* I think everything is great. I think life is great and there's a lot to be happy and excited about. Somehow I just knew I could license my own ideas. When I went down to the store and looked at the products there, I knew I could do better. I was not impressed with the existing products on the shelf. I'd also worked for a company and watched it license ideas from creative people like Ken Forsse.

My attitude set me apart from classic inventors. In the early days, I didn't network much with other product designers. I still don't think of myself as an inventor, because I have never really identified with that word. I don't fit the typical image of an inventor. I'm a social creature and not one to squirrel myself away in a garage to tinker. But since other people tended to call me an inventor, I decided to check out different inventors' associations.

At my first inventors' association meeting, I felt confused. I wasn't having any of the problems with which these people were obsessed. Inventors often start by seeing a problem and visualizing a solution. That's all well and good. But that orientation tends to fixate many of them on the problems themselves. Their meetings get gobbled up by debates about finding investors and spending years and thousands of dollars on patents.

I tell my inventRight students not to waste their time on prototypes and patents. When you license, it's not that complicated. To successfully license, you don't even need big ideas. Small ones will do. Slight or incremental changes translate most rapidly and most profitably to market. And to find them, you do not have to be an inventor.

First and foremost, I am a consumer. I'm the kind of guy who likes to go to stores and look around at all the fun stuff you can buy. Maybe this describes you. Do you like to shop for electronic gadgets? Cosmetics? Toys? Tools? Kitchenware? Or any other kind of stuff? If so, then you are qualified to dream up ideas for new and renewed products and then license them.

Welcome to the New World of Innovation

You may have heard it said that inventors are our most valuable resource. I say ideas are our most valuable resource. If we are going to solve some of the world's most vexing problems, from saving the environment to curing diseases, the answers are going to come through new thinking. Very few products are manufactured in the West anymore, but we do produce exceptional ideas. What a lot of people don't realize is that there is a new and much simpler way to get those great ideas from conception to market. And anyone can do it—including you. Especially you, if you're a creative type who dreams of being an entrepreneur steering your own ship and controlling your own destiny.

One of the best things about this new world of innovation is that today you can build a career, or at least a hobby, on the single most exciting aspect of any business: creating ideas. All you need is a passion for good products or services.

Now I'm going to explain something to you that most "experts" just don't get. My livelihood and the courses I teach are based on a single word you have heard before and read in these very pages, but may not understand: *licensing*. Licensing is currently a huge industry. In the United States for example it is worth $500 billion to the economy. That's bigger than the cell phone and magazine publishing industries combined. I predict that number will only grow.

In basic terms, licensing means taking your idea, your "intellectual property," and giving someone with a lot of powerful resources the privilege of using it for a price. You set the terms by which you extend this privilege. In return, they give you a rent check, also known as a "royalty" check, four times a year. These quarterly royalty checks, and sometimes one-time advances on future royalties, are the means by which you will generate income. Sometime a royalty check is $1,000. Sometimes it's $10,000, or $100,000, or $1 million. I have students who bring in millions in royalty income. I have many others who make $30,000 to $40,000 a year for each of their three licenses for a total annual income of $90,000 to $120,000. Not bad.

Still with me? If you graduated from a top business university or college, you may not be. Graduates of top institutions have been mercilessly drilled in the ways of the Old World, the world of manufacturing. That means they can't separate the concept of renting their ideas—or anyone else's—from the unexamined conviction that they have to go out and start their own company to do so. They don't know there's another way to be entrepreneurial. They have invested a tremendous amount of tuition and mental energy into figuring out how to raise money from venture capitalists or angel investors or how to get a loan from a bank or the Small Business Administration or a wealthy aunt. Or they may already be bootstrapping to fund their company's growth through cash flow. To keep on growing, they will have to become expert at managing people, sourcing material, running faster and more efficiently than the competition, generating cash flow, minimizing the tax bill, and keeping down costs like rent, electricity, payroll, and legal fees.

There's nothing wrong with doing all that work if you've got the passion and aptitude for it. But maybe you don't. Even if you do have what it takes to launch and run a company, your business may still fail miserably, regardless of the merit of your idea. Businesses owned by well-educated and competent people fail all the time, sometimes because they were unable to do all those complex tasks as well as they'd hoped. Sometimes it's because they put all their eggs into one basket, focusing all of their resources on a single product or brand. And sometimes it's because their idea wasn't so great after all, which is often the result of creating a product for which there wasn't a good market. These are the sad stories you won't find recounted on the pages of business magazines.

I'm acquainted with a professor at one of America's top universities. He developed a product and raised millions from investors to start a company, only to find 10 years later that there was no market for it. Today he wishes he had figured this out before he invested not only his own lifeblood and resources but also his investors' resources in a venture that was doomed to fail from the outset. It's a fitting commentary that this individual, though highly intelligent and entirely well-meaning, is no longer an entrepreneur, but a professor teaching others.

If he had used my system for creating and bringing ideas to market, he might have discovered the flaws in his strategy long before so many resources were lost. If you decide to start a company to bring your ideas to market, you can still use my road map for rapidly testing the marketability of an idea to save yourself years and, literally, millions of dollars worth of trouble.

Not long ago, I was invited to talk to students at the renowned School of Design at Stanford University. Aspiring engineers and industrial designers come there from all over the world to learn the most cutting-edge technologies and techniques. They pay a fortune in tuition for the privilege of learning how to turn their brilliant ideas (and many of them are, indeed, mind-blowing) into market successes. But they are so focused on doing it the old way that they couldn't hear me when I started explaining what I do. Instead, they looked at me as if I had a third eye. (Although, afterward, many of them called me asking for advice.)

Another time, I spoke to the employees of one of the premier industrial design firms in the country. I doubt I will be asked back. Naturally, companies want to hang on to their best people. In effect, I showed all their brilliant designers the keys to escape the prison of employment. I explained exactly how to bring their ideas to market and cut their employer out of the process.

The amount of time and resources devoted to educating some of the smartest minds out there about the Old World way of bringing products to market is so exhaustive, so overwhelming, that many very bright people just can't conceive of there being an easier way to do this. I suspect that to them, licensing seems like cheating. After all, they're already accustomed to working long hours and getting little sleep, to spending a lot of money, and to working very, *very* hard. They can't imagine there is another way to realize their entrepreneurial dreams that might be . . . easier, faster, simpler.

That's exactly what the licensing lifestyle can be: *simple*. And it all begins, and continues, with *one simple idea*.

2

The Beauty—and Opportunity—of Open Innovation

For more than a decade I've been teaching other people how to license their ideas—now it's your turn. And your timing couldn't be better! Licensing your ideas has become easier than ever, thanks to the Internet as well as to new tools and strategies that enable you to bypass the prototype and patent processes (which you'll read about in Chapter 11). But the most significant element driving the modern licensing wave is the innovation-driven global marketplace that has changed the way companies do business.

Companies of all sizes and in all industries have realized that to stay in the game, in some cases just to stay alive, they must innovate continually and quickly. Given the exorbitant costs of traditional research and development (R&D) and the economic constraints facing almost every company today, few can afford to develop all of their products and processes internally and at the pace required.

Besides, although many "insiders" are reluctant to admit it, today many of the most innovative and successful ideas come from the "outside"—from people like you and me, the ones who actually buy and use all this stuff. As I'm sure you've noticed, there is more stuff in the market all the time—exponentially more every year.

Finally, and this is pivotal, it is often much faster and more economical for a company to bring to market a licensed product *based on a simple idea*—an improvement or enhancement to an existing product—than it is to start at square one in R&D and go through the whole long, complicated, and expensive process of coming up with and developing an idea themselves.

So licensing our ideas is really just good business for companies. It reduces their R&D costs. It accelerates their product development time. And it creates a multiplying effect: essentially getting other people to develop ideas for them for free.

This concept of companies licensing ideas from outside their own walls, otherwise known as *open innovation*, was unheard of when I first entered the licensing game. Twenty years ago, Procter & Gamble (P&G) would never have given me the time of day. Now, P&G—the largest consumer products company in the world—is among the vanguards of the open-innovation movement. Nine years ago, P&G set a goal of sourcing at least half of their new products from the outside. A few years later, they reached that goal. In 2009, more than 100 of the new products that P&G released came from outside ideas. As Jeff Weedman, a P&G vice president involved with the company's open-innovation strategy, has said: "We don't care where good ideas come from as long as they come to us."

P&G is not alone. Today, the world's most enlightened corporations, including Black & Decker, Ford, Kraft Foods, Samsung Electronics, and thousands upon thousands of others, have opened their doors to outside innovators.

The Global Churn

Innovation is driving the global economy. A hot new product comes out in the United States or the United Kingdom, in Japan or Germany, and thanks largely to the Internet, it's soon selling in all four corners of the world. No sooner does the latest product or process hit the market than someone somewhere is upping the ante: creating a new and improved spin-off; adapting it for new applications or for new demographic, geographic, or niche markets; making it better, fancier, simpler, cheaper, prettier, "greener," improving it in some beneficial and simple way.

The Opportunity

It used to be that a country's manufacturing capacity determined its dominance in the global economy: the higher a country's gross domestic product (GDP), the bigger its share of the global market. Not anymore. Today, the countries that dominate the world economy are the ones that produce the most ideas. In other words, the more *intellectual property* a country controls, the bigger its slice of the global market pie.

Intellectual property is the legal ownership, by a company or individual, of an *intangible asset*, a creation of the mind—an idea. Intellectual property encompasses many types of intangible assets, including musical, literary, and other artistic works; ideas, discoveries, and inventions; and words, phrases, symbols, and designs. The owner of intellectual property has the right to produce and market the creation, or to grant someone else the right, the license, to produce and market it for them.

The reason the United States still owns the biggest share of the global market is because U.S. companies own or control most of the world's intellectual property. Although little manufacturing is actually done in the United States, the country's GDP remains the largest in the world and not by a small margin. It is three times larger than that of Japan (the second largest GDP in the world) and four times larger than Germany's and China's. So the United States is responsible for most of the world's innovation *and* sells most of the goods and services derived from those innovations around the world.

Not only does the United States control the lion's share of the world's intellectual property, it is also a huge market *for* the tangible manifestations of those ideas. The United States is a major, if not *the* major, consumer of products, services, processes, and technologies on the planet. And we don't just buy and use innovations created by U.S. minds and companies. We also consume innovations from minds and companies around the world.

So today's innovations are coming from all over the world and are consumed all over the world. The innovation wheel just keeps churning, forcing companies to innovate constantly and quickly. To keep up, many companies have opened their doors to outside innovators. That has created a world of opportunity for independent product developers like you and me.

The Beauty

Not only does the global churn of open innovation provide entrepreneurs and independent innovators like you and me with a huge opportunity, it also gives us a distinct advantage. Why? For these three reasons:

1. We're close to the market.
2. We're creative and motivated.
3. We're quick on our feet.

First and foremost, as consumers we know what we like and don't like. We know what's out there in the market. We also know what *isn't* out there and should be. As entrepreneurs we thrive on creating new ideas and improving on existing ideas. We're motivated to bring our ideas to market, to share them with the world and to benefit personally from them. Since we don't have a big company to run and worry about, we can turn on a dime to bring those ideas to life (so that a licensee can quickly bring them to market). We don't have the overhead and the hierarchy to impede our creativity and progress. We don't have to form a committee, or jump through hoops, or finance a long, drawn-out process to develop a product, build a prototype, get a patent, and secure the buy-in of different departments and investors.

Now here's the beauty of this new world of open innovation: it doesn't have to be a big idea. It can be a simple idea or a simple improvement to a product that's already out there. Piggybacking on existing products gives you a real advantage. You don't have to educate the world about your idea. You don't have to create a market for it; there already *is* a market for it. You don't have to invent or reinvent something brand new. It's your shortest, fastest route to licensing success. Because a simple improvement or a small incremental change to an existing product is often the easiest, fastest, most cost-effective, and most profitable way for companies to bring a new product to market.

You might think they would have come up with these simple ideas themselves, but they often don't. I truly believe that sometimes these big companies are so close to *what is* that they don't even consider *what if*. It sometimes appears as if they wouldn't know a good idea if it hit them on the head. With all their departments and committees, I think it's hard for them to think outside the box or even right beside the box, which is where many of the most doable and profitable ideas are situated. In many of these companies, one person knows one thing and another knows another thing, but nobody knows the entire process—nobody has the whole story.

As a consumer and an innovator, you not only have the larger perspective, but you also know how your idea fits into the big picture. You know the market, and you start at the beginning of the innovation process: with an idea.

There are so many ideas out there waiting for you to find them. You just have to look at things a little differently. Take a close look at the products you use at home, at play, in the ads in magazines. Keep your eyes open and look for a simple idea that you feel passionate about. If you're passionate about it, chances are you'll be able to "innovate right" and get a company passionate about licensing it.

That brings me to another beautiful thing about open innovation: it's a one-size-fits-all strategy. Companies of all shapes and sizes are potential licensees for your idea. That said, a midsize company is usually the ideal candidate to license your idea. They have the money, and they are most likely to view the licensing of an idea as an opportunity to become number two or three in the market. Small companies are the least likely to have the capital and other resources to bring your idea to market. Although some really big companies do license ideas, they are more likely to *buy* ideas that are developed outside their walls than they are to *rent* them. When a big corporation is interested in an idea created by an independent product developer or a design firm, they typically want to purchase the idea (patents) outright. Likewise, if they're interested in an idea that a smaller company has developed, they typically just buy the other company.

So I suggest you find the number three or number four player in the market and show them how licensing your idea can make them number two or even number one. But don't rule out any company based on size alone. Any company that sells in your product category is a potential licensee; you just need to find the right company to license your idea, which you'll learn about in Chapter 16.

First to Market Wins

The same forces that are fueling the global churn of innovation—technology, the Internet, consumerism—have also shortened the "legs" of those very innovations. Today, new products sweep in and out of the market at a dizzying pace. The life cycle of any given product is shorter than ever, and the window of opportunity to get an idea to market is shrinking. In this environment, the first to market wins.

It's All About Shelf Space

Forget prototypes! Forget patents! Forget venturing!

What matters most in today's innovation-driven global economy is *shelf space*—getting your idea in front of consumers before someone else beats you to it. The easiest and fastest way to get your idea to market is to license it to a company that already has shelf space at Walmart, Kroger, Best Buy, Cabela's, Home Depot, Toys "R" Us, or wherever consumers shop for whatever you dream up.

Of course, your idea doesn't have to be for a consumer product. It can be for a product or process purchased and used by businesses, governments, scientists, and so on. Personally, though, I think dreaming up ideas for consumer products is fun, and the opportunities for innovation are endless. Consumer spending accounts for 60 to 70 percent of the total U.S. economy, even during economic slumps, and 40 percent of consumer spending is discretionary and driven by desire, not necessity. Figures in the U.K. and Canada tell a similar story. When consumers want something, they want it now, not years from now. Consumers in the commercial, government, and scientific sectors are no more patient.

Say you go the conventional route of bringing an idea to market. While you're spending all your time and money building prototypes and getting patents; writing a business plan, raising capital, setting up and running a company; and muscling your way into retailers and wrestling shelf space away from established companies, you can believe that someone else is going to bring your idea, or something close enough to it, to market. Bam! Your window of opportunity has just been slammed shut.

Licensing your ideas to established companies puts your idea on the fast track to market. It gets you shelf space now. Plus, it shifts all the costs and risks of bringing your idea to market to the licensee, and there are *always* risks associated with bringing products to market, especially new ones.

The Tao of Now

Successful companies of all sizes know the importance of shelf space. They also know shelf space for "me too" products is extremely limited, that some wholesalers and retailers want nothing whatsoever to do with them. They know many consumers feel the same way: they want only the real deal, the name brands, the firsts to market.

So to secure shelf space for their products and to ensure continued shelf space for future products, smart companies strive to continually innovate, to be *first movers*, to always stay ahead of the competition. By being the first to market, they grab shelf space, and with it, market share. To keep and grow their shelf space and market share, they continue to innovate, continue to be first to market.

These companies realize that open innovation—licensing ideas from the outside—enables them to be first to market and to fill their shelf space with products consumers want. Believe me, these companies want your ideas. They *need* your ideas. They benefit from your ideas. More important, licensing your ideas benefits *you*. It enables you to be a first mover: to get your idea on the market before someone else comes out with a similar idea.

The conventional method of bringing an idea to market—building prototypes, getting patents, building a company around it, and so on—takes so much time, money, and effort that, in my opinion and experience, it just doesn't make sense for most ideas. When you license your idea to a company, everything is already in place. You just plug into their product line, and you're ready to rock and roll. They take care of manufacturing, marketing, sales, distribution, customer service, and all that other business. You collect royalty checks, *and* you still own the idea.

Licensing is the easiest and fastest way to get your idea on the shelf . . . and to start generating income for you.

HOW A SIMPLE SCREW MADE MILLIONS

Dwight Deveraux contacted me several years ago, wondering whether I could help him with his idea. A former guitarist for the 1980s pop-rock band Tommy Tutone (you may remember the group's Billboard Top 40's hits "867-5309/Jenny" and "Angel Say No") and a guitar aficionado, Dwight had developed a "locking stud" that kept a guitar's bridge from falling off when replacing the strings and also improved the intonation and "sustain" of the strings. He had run the idea by a luthier, or guitar maker, Kurt Laubhan, and Kurt helped him build a prototype. A friend of a friend referred Dwight to me, because he had some questions about whether he should protect his idea, how to go about doing it, and how to bring his idea to market.

I met with Dwight at his home—something I never do, but I did it this time because he was both a friend of a friend and my neighbor, and he had a physical impairment that limited his mobility. He explained that with existing technology, when you removed the strings to replace them, the bridge (the metal plate on the guitar's body to which all the strings are attached) often would fall off. As you replaced the strings, you had to hold the bridge in place with one hand while attaching new strings with the other. This made restringing a guitar difficult and time-consuming, and when the bridge fell off, it often scratched the guitar's surface.

Then Dwight showed me how his idea solved this problem: First, you replaced the two screws (called studs) on either side of the wraparound bridge with the special "locking" screws that Dwight had designed. To replace the strings, you loosened the studs enough to remove and replace the strings, but the screws stayed locked in place, preventing the bridge from falling off. Once you had replaced all the strings, you tightened the studs, tuned your guitar, adjusted the pressure of the studs on the bridge to achieve the perfect intonation, and were ready to play within a few minutes.

His idea was so simple. Dwight wondered: *Did it have value? Could he protect it?* Absolutely, I assured him. In fact, his idea was simply genius!

I then explained my process for developing, protecting, and licensing ideas. I connected Dwight with the right attorneys, told him the right questions to ask, and gave him my road map for licensing his idea—the same one I've used successfully. The same one you're learning about in this book.

In 1998, Dwight started licensing his locking screws to guitar component manufacturers. Peter Wiltz, a longtime friend and a renowned guitar tech who toured with artists such as Bruce Springsteen, the Eagles, and the Rolling Stones, was instrumental in getting Dwight's locking studs into the hands of the world's top guitarists. Today, Dwight's company, TonePros, both manufactures the locking studs and licenses them to manufacturers—to the same companies that supply parts to the top guitar manufacturers in the world, such as Gibson and Fender. TonePros locking studs are distributed to more than 30 countries on four continents.

Dwight has said that his "playing career does not rival the success of TonePros." But his simple idea has enabled him to live a very comfortable lifestyle, to continue being an integral part of the music industry, and to make a major contribution to the instrument he loves.

In one way, Dwight's story is unique. Few of us have the resources, skill set, and desire needed to successfully manufacture, market, and distribute our ideas. In another way, Dwight's story is similar to mine and to anyone's who has created and licensed an idea. And it could be your story, because a huge component of Dwight's success is that he came up with a simple idea that he was able to license to other companies that had a *much* bigger share of the market than his little company did.

Today, thousands of companies around the world—from midsized manufacturers to megacorporations—are looking for the same kind of simple ideas. The need and opportunity for open innovation has never been greater. With the tools and techniques you'll find in this book, it has never been easier to create and license ideas. Now is the perfect time for you to jump into the open-innovation game!

3

CEO or CIO—Which Hat Fits You Best?

*I*DEAS ARE *a dime a dozen.* So goes the old maxim. There is a hard truth to that. An idea has little value in the real world until it is actually *in* the real world—selling in the marketplace, benefitting consumers in some way, and generating revenue for whoever owns and manufactures it. There are basically two ways to get your idea to market: do it yourself or get a company to do it for you.

Doing it yourself means starting a new business, or if you already own a business, adapting and expanding it, to develop, manufacture, market, sell, and distribute the product or process. That's the chief executive officer (CEO) hat. Of course, with most start-ups, the founder/owner of the company wears multiple hats: CEO, chief operating officer (COO), chief financial officer (CFO), vice president (VP) of product development, VP of marketing and sales, director of distribution, director of human resources, and many more. With the manufacturing route to market, you assume all the responsibilities, risks, and costs. You also reap all the profits—or eat all the losses, as is often the case.

With licensing, you are the chief innovation officer (CIO) of your *idea* rather than the CEO of your *business*. You wear one hat: the creative one. Your primary focus is to bring your idea to life and license it to an existing company that brings it to market. The licensee, rather than you, assumes all the responsibilities, risks, and costs of manufacturing and selling the product. They pay you a percentage of sales, or a *royalty*, in exchange for renting your idea.

Neither approach is superior or inferior to the other. With some ideas, manufacturing the product yourself is the better way to get your idea to market. With other ideas, licensing is the better route. In fact, I believe licensing is a much better, faster, easier, and cheaper route to market for *most* ideas conjured up by entrepreneurs, independent product developers, and regular people who use these products every day and come up with innovative ways to improve them. For people like me, whose interests and capabilities align more closely with creating new products than with running a business, licensing is also a more gratifying way to get an idea to market.

Let's face it, not everyone is cut out to be a CEO. Not everyone has the abilities, resources, and desire to start, manage, and grow a business. But everyone can come up with a simple idea that companies will want to produce and consumers will want to buy.

Of course, not all ideas are created equal, either. Some ideas are too complicated or too new or too expensive for a company to want to take on, leaving you no choice but to bring it to market yourself . . . or to let it go. On the flip side, some ideas are or seem so easy to make and sell that you'll want to do it yourself, and sometimes that works out just fine.

CEO or CIO: how do you decide which hat fits you and your idea? Well, that depends largely on your interests, capabilities, resources, and the idea itself. It also depends on the market. There is no simple formula for delineating the ideal scenario for licensing versus the ideal scenario for manufacturing. But you can keep this formula in mind as a rule of thumb:

Simple idea + existing technology + 3 or more players in the market = license

Unique idea + new technology + 1 or 2 major players in market = manufacture

Knowing what's involved with each approach will also help you determine whether manufacturing or licensing is the best route to market for your idea.

Manufacturing 101

Starting a manufacturing company requires a lot of expertise, money, work, and time, no matter how simple your idea may be. Unless you've done it before and unless you're already a major player in the market, it typically takes years and hundreds of thousands, if not millions, of dollars to get a company going and a new product to market—and even longer to turn a profit, if you ever do. According to the latest statistics from the U.S. Small Business Administration (SBA), one-third of new "employer enterprises" (businesses with employees) fail within the first two years and more than half fail within the first four years. But even if your business is among the 66 percent that makes it past the two-year mark and the 34 percent that makes it beyond four years, you still have to go through the same start-up process and take on the same risks as the businesses that ultimately fail. And it's not a walk in the park.

Here are the major steps involved in bringing your idea to market yourself:

- **Study the market.** The absolute first thing you'll need to do is determine whether there *is* a market for your product as well as who your target customers are, who your competitors are, and what your product offers consumers that your competition does not.
- **Develop the product.** This typically involves designing the product and the packaging, building and testing prototypes, and filing a patent.
- **Determine how to manufacture the product.** What materials, processes, technologies, skilled labor, facilities, and equipment will be required to produce and distribute your product? Who are your potential vendors? What local, state, and national rules and regulations will you need to comply with? Manufacturers pay 81 percent more in regulatory costs than do other types of businesses; you'll need to know these requirements and costs up front.
- **Write a business plan.** This comprehensive document proves on paper that a viable market exists for your product, that your busi-

ness is capable of producing and selling the product, and that you can sell enough of the product to be profitable and to be attractive to potential backers. It must include a production and distribution plan, a marketing and sales plan, and a slew of financial data and projections.

- **Put up and raise capital.** Getting even a small manufacturing company up and running is likely to cost hundreds of thousands of dollars—more than most people can get from investors, mortgaging their homes, or borrowing money from banks, friends, and relatives. Not surprisingly, inadequate funding is the leading cause of business failure.
- **Launch the company.** You'll need licenses, insurance, facilities, and at least a few employees. You'll also need to purchase equipment and materials to make, package, and distribute your product.
- **Sell the hell out of the product.** When you're the new kid on a block dominated by heavy hitters, this is much easier said than done. No matter how brilliant your idea and how many resources you throw at advertising, marketing, trade shows, and sales—and you'll need to do all of that—it is always tough to break into a market, much less to grab a big-enough share of it fast enough to survive.
- **Keep up with the market.** Remember the global churn you read about in Chapter 2? Well, that whirling dervish is always on your tail, forcing you either to stay abreast of market trends or to go out of business. Innovate or become obsolete: that's the new rule of the game.

Any way you cut it, manufacturing is a tough row to hoe, and it isn't for everybody. But when it works for you and your idea, it gives you maximum control of the product, the process, and profits.

Licensing: Easy as 1-2-3

The first phase in the licensing route to market is actually the same as in the manufacturing route: *study the market.* The more you know about the market, the more likely you are to design a product that companies will want to license and consumers will want to buy. Do some market research. Do some comparative shopping.

At the very least, you must find the answers to these six critical questions:

1. Who are my competitors? Identify both the major players and the smaller players.
2. How does my idea compare and contrast with other products in the market?
3. What value does it offer that the other products do not?
4. How large is the market?
5. Who are my primary customers?
6. What are my potential sales?

The second phase in the licensing process is to *develop your product*, or what I like to call "bringing your idea to life." This involves translating your idea into a bona fide product and proving that it's doable, valuable, and sellable. As with manufacturing, this may require building and testing a prototype and filing a patent. But it doesn't have to. Not if it's a simple idea: an improvement, enhancement, or incremental change to an existing product with a proven market. Not if it's a simple idea that uses existing technology. Instead of a prototype, a concept drawing or a computer model will likely do the trick. (You'll learn all about prototypes and other ways to model your ideas in Chapter 10.) You should also know the basics of manufacturing the product, so that you can speak intelligently about it to potential licensees.

You will need some sort of intellectual property protection for your idea, but filing a patent is not your only option. I am not an attorney and cannot give legal advice, but here is what has worked for me and hundreds of other independent product developers: file a provisional patent application. It will give you patent pending for one year without huge expenditures of time and money, and you can even file it yourself. (I will tell you how in Chapter 11.)

The third phase is to *secure a licensing contract*. This involves identifying potential licensees and picking the right one, which is what Chapter 16 is about. It also involves getting your foot in the door and licensing your idea to those companies—which I cover in Chapter 17. The important thing to remember is that you're selling the *benefit* of your idea, which you can usually accomplish with a good concept drawing (or computer model) along with a hard-hitting benefit statement and a great sell sheet, which I talk about in Chapter 13. Then it's simply a matter of cutting a great deal, and I tell you how to do that in Chapter 18.

In fact, I wrote this book to show you how easy it is to license your ideas. It's certainly a whole lot easier—and in my opinion, a lot more fun—than launching a company to bring an idea to market. I know this to be true from my own firsthand experience—in licensing more than 20 of my ideas and manufacturing one, and only one, ever.

MY ONE FORAY INTO MANUFACTURING

About five years ago, a longtime friend of mine named Rob came to me with a proposition. We both knew a guy who was making a slew of money selling a guitar pick with the image of an alien head printed on it. Rob wanted to do something similar. I thought about it for a minute, because the last thing I wanted to do was get into a business. But this was a creative challenge. So I said, "Why not?"

The first thing I did was go to the mall to check out the images kids liked. One of the stores I browsed was Hot Topic. Now, if you're familiar with Hot Topic, you can imagine how out-of-place a 50-year-old man looked in a dark store that was blasting loud alternative rock music and filled with teens and tweens wearing black Goth clothing, with every imaginable part of their bodies pierced. But it worked. I noticed that the most popular products in the store had skulls on them. One sticker in particular stood out: it was in the shape of a skull, but the chin came to a point. Instantly, it looked like a guitar pick to me. The light went on: rather than just printing an image on the surface, why not change the shape of the pick, too? Just a little bit. As long as the picks were the standard sizes and thicknesses and were in the basic shape of a rounded triangle, why couldn't they be shaped like skulls, or hearts, or alien heads—or for that matter, Mickey Mouse (which by the way, we eventually licensed from Disney)?

We had some skull picks made and took them to the largest music trade show in America, where we gave away the Grave Picker, as we called it. Our booth was packed. I knew then and there we had a hit.

But I also knew, from my market research, that the two companies dominating the market would never license my idea, because it was too novel and the owners were guitar players. You see, guitar picks had been the same shape for 80 years. I do not play the guitar, but Rob does. At first, he thought my idea was nuts, too. But then he saw that it worked, and he knew it would sell. Because he had had a music store for 15 years, he also knew all the distributors. We figured the picks would cost only pennies to make, and we even knew a guy in town who could make them for us. A million picks could fit under my desk, so storing inventory wouldn't be a problem. I could do the designs; Rob could do the selling. How hard could it be?

Hard. Very hard. I've never worked harder in my life. I worked six long days a week. I had to wear many different hats. It took about a quarter million dollars to get the company up and running. We had no idea it was going to cost that much and be that much work. Making and selling a few guitar picks out of your garage is one thing. But to be successful, we had to produce and sell large volumes. We ended up in over ten thousand stores worldwide. HotPicks became a big player in a small industry in a short period of time. I had a blast! I got to work with some great bands and great people, like Taylor Swift and her family. And I had complete control.

But it took $250,000, a time frame of more than a year, and a lot of blood, sweat, and tears to get there. In comparison, I can develop a product for licensing in less than 30 days and for under $500—which I had already done successfully 20 times . . . and had a fantastic time doing it.

With HotPicks, I had stopped being creative and was just running a business. It got to be not so much fun. So I sold the company to Rob and some investors and went back to innovating and licensing my ideas, which fits me to a tee.

As you can see, from my experience licensing takes a heck of a lot less time, effort, and money than launching and running a manufacturing company does. Dollar for dollar, hour for hour, and task for task, licensing is a cheaper, faster, and easier way to get your idea to market. True, you lose some control, but you gain the freedom to create even *more* great ideas. You also have the freedom to live and work wherever you choose. Even though you get a smaller share of profits, you have a *lot less to do* and a *lot less to lose*. And licensing can be very lucrative. Just ask the thousands of people, like me, who are enjoying the licensing lifestyle.

You can, too. All you need is one simple idea.

PART TWO

Find Your Million-Dollar Idea

Do you frequently think of ideas for new and better products and wish, *If only I could make a living doing this!*

Have you ever felt frustrated because you can't find the perfect product and wondered, *Why doesn't someone come up with a product that is exactly what you're looking for?*

When you hear about someone who has come up with a simple idea that forever changed his life for the better, do you think, *Why can't I do something like that?*

Well, you can. Anyone can. Great ideas are everywhere, hiding in plain sight. You just need to know where to find them and how to mine them.

4

Look for Marketable Ideas

M OST PEOPLE innovate backward. They develop a product to solve a problem that bothers them personally without first confirming that it bothers the market universally. They dream up a product without first identifying who will use it, how, and why. They conjure up a clever idea—thinking, *Man, this is going to be mind-blowing! Nothing like it out there!* Then they build a prototype, file a patent, and start making and marketing it—without first identifying the market, qualifying the market, or even knowing whether there *is* a market for it.

Not surprisingly, most of those ideas fail. In fact, most patents never make more money than the cost of the patent itself. Why? Primarily because the designer innovated for the sake of innovation rather than for the benefit of the market.

There is a better way to innovate. It is this simple: instead of creating a new market for your idea, create an idea for an *existing* market. In my experience and the experience of countless others, the fastest, easiest, and most profitable road to licensing success is with an evolutionary idea, not a revolutionary one. It's with giving a new twist, a small tweak, or a unique value to a proven product. It's with a simple idea.

But don't mistake simple for mundane. In today's global churn, where innovation is the order of the day, creativity is king. Whatever your idea is, it has to stand out in the marketplace. It has to offer something that competitors don't *and* consumers want. It has to have that touch of creative genius.

Don't let that scare you, though. Virtually anyone can come up with a simple but creative idea that has great licensing potential. Sure, coming up with novel ideas comes naturally to some people. They look at a glob of bread dough and see Play-Doh. They see a child trip over his untied shoelaces and instantly think, *Velcro ties!* They look at an ID tag that's slipped off a dog collar and think, *pet microchip!* But most people need to look harder and longer at many things for an idea to materialize.

No matter how creative you are or are not, there are tools and methods you can use to find marketable ideas.

A Few Practical Tips

Ideas can come from many different places and at any time. I get some of my best ideas when I'm driving and, of course, when I'm shopping. For some people, their most creative ideas come when they're taking a shower or bath or while going for a walk. Some prefer retreating to a quiet place that blocks out distractions; others are more creative in the thick of things, where their ideas can cross-pollinate with whatever is going on around them.

Nobody creates in a vacuum, though. Everybody needs inspiration and information to come up with marketable ideas. Trust me, you'll be doing a lot of researching, brainstorming, gathering information, asking questions, making observations, taking photos, sketching out your ideas, and checking out lots of different things. So you'll need some basic tools for collecting all of that information.

Here are a few simple suggestions:

- Keep your iPad, Blackberry, or other mobile note-taking device, or even a small paper notebook and a couple of pens, with you wherever you go.
- Take a small digital camera shopping with you or a smart phone. As they say, a picture is worth a thousand words. With a smart

phone, you can take a photo of an interesting product and add a few notes about it in a heartbeat.

- Keep a small audio recorder in your car, so you can record your ideas without looking away from the road to jot them down. If the shower or bathtub is your creativity hub of choice, keep the recorder within arm's reach (but don't get it wet). Again, a smart phone or other mobile device with the ability to audio record and replay is a great all-in-one tool for researching marketable ideas.

- Keep a drawing pad and some pencils wherever you brainstorm and work on your ideas. Some people can electronically "draw" their ideas on a computer or mobile device. I prefer to sketch out my ideas by hand.

- Keep all the information for your idea in one place. That includes anything that inspires you or helps stimulate your creativity.

- Ideally, you'll also have a Web-enabled computer, iPad, or similar mobile device. The Internet is a great market-research tool. The amount of information on the Web today is astounding, and most of it is free. I rely heavily—although never exclusively—on information I find online.

OK, now that you've got the basic tools of the trade in place, it's time to find a market that gets your creative motor running.

Study the Marketplace

It's one thing to create a product you like. It's quite another to design a product that consumers like and will buy. Companies are only interested in licensing ideas they're convinced will sell. To be convinced of that, they must see not only how the idea fits into the market but also how it is unique. If there are too many products similar to yours and your idea doesn't offer a truly unique value, the market may be too saturated to allow room for your idea. On the other hand, if there are no products similar to yours out there, there may not be a viable market for your idea.

That's why it's vitally important to study the market. It is the best way to figure out which market you want to work in, to brainstorm ideas that will sell in that market, and to design your idea *for* the market.

The most marketable ideas are those that solve problems, address needs, or satisfy desires. In other words, they provide value that the consumer is willing to pay for. When I came up with the idea for the Michael Jordan Wall Ball, I knew kids didn't need it. It didn't solve a problem; there were other inside basketball games on the market that worked fine. But there weren't any indoor basketball hoops with Michael Jordan's image on them, and I knew kids would want one.

Large companies spend millions of dollars on market research trying to identify consumer wants, needs, and problems and to generate ideas for meeting them. I just went to Toys "R" Us and walked the aisles. I love basketball, so I checked out all the basketball stuff. I looked at what was on the shelves and tried to imagine ways to make a small change that would have a big impact. I also observed how kids responded to the basketball products on the shelves, and it didn't take long to see that they loved anything with Michael Jordan on it.

Of course, my shopping excursions only planted the seed of an idea. I had to do more market research to germinate that idea: to figure out how to design it, how much it should cost, who might license it, and so on. But all of my market research was free. All it took was some ingenuity and some of my time.

You can do the same thing. You can study the marketplace, first to find a market or product category to design for and then to come up with an innovative idea *for* that market. You can't rely on assumptions and guesses; you need real-world information.

Here are several ways to research the market:

- Scout the marketplace to discover hot markets and emerging trends. Check out websites (such as Trendsetter.com and Mind Branch.com), blogs, social networking groups, online forums, trade and consumer magazines, TV shows, and industry newsletters that focus on or cover market trends. Go shopping, look at new products, and ask store managers which items are hot.

- Learn as much as you can about a specific market: customer demographics, the companies providing most of the products, the range of products within the market, and so on.
- Check out existing products in the market; assess their features and functions, strengths and weaknesses, prices and popularity.
- Evaluate how your idea stacks up against the competition; figure out your idea's unique value proposition: what it offers that comparative products do not.
- Figure out where your idea fits into the market: determine who will buy your product, how they will use it, where they will buy it, and how much they might pay for it.
- Find out how your idea might be manufactured and packaged.
- Determine the manufacturing price point as well as the retail price point.

To gather this information, you don't have to go through the long, complicated, and expensive market-research process that companies go through. There are simple ways for you to study the market—and they're free.

Go Shopping

If you're fishing for a market that's rich with innovation opportunities, cast a wide net and see what you come up with. Go to the mall and big-box general retailers, like Walmart and Target, and walk the aisles. Go to specialty stores that carry products you're interested in or curious about. Take your time and really look at the merchandise. Ask the store manager or store clerks which products are new, which are selling well, and which are duds. Take note of products customers are drooling over and buying—and which they're passing over.

If you find yourself being drawn to a certain product or product category, focus on that area of the store. Examine the products more closely. Check out variations in design, quality, size, packaging, and price. Notice which products have the most shelf space and the most prominent displays. Take notes and photos of products that pique your interest or that you sense offer innovation opportunities.

Although I personally think that in-store visits are invaluable to a product designer, you don't have to go to a brick-and-mortar store to do your market research. You can research the market by browsing consumer magazines, catalogs, and the Internet. In fact, I usually do both online and in-store market-shopping. All of the major retailers have online stores, and there are innumerable online specialty stores and shopping hubs.

Once you've settled on a market and come up with a rough idea of a product for that market, go shopping again. Go to the sections of the store where products similar to your idea are sold. Check out all of the products in that area. Which are the most and least expensive? What are the features and functions of each product? What is each product's most unique and desirable characteristic? What is its least desirable characteristic? How is each product packaged and displayed? How might your product fit into this market and on which shelf? How does your idea compare and contrast with other products in the market?

Again, talk to the store manager or clerks and ask questions. Observe customers. Make notes and take photos. Most store managers won't care if you take photos, and you can always say you're collecting ideas for birthday or Christmas gifts. Chances are, if you're discreet in taking a few photos using your small phone or a small digital camera, no one will even notice.

With most products, especially at this stage of the design process, you can usually rely on in-store visits and browsing the online stores of big-box retailers and the major specialty stores in a given market. Other great places to "shop" for ideas include mail-order catalogs, TV shopping shows, and online shopping portals for certain product categories.

Sometimes, I also use two different Google searches for whatever product I'm working on. Let's say, for example, I have an idea for a new twist on an old tool—the hammer. Here's what I would do:

- **Go to http://www.google.com/images.** Click on Advanced Image Search, type in a few keywords, and define a few other parameters for my hammer-image search. Scan the search results, clicking on any image that seems relevant to my idea. In many cases, when that links to a Web page, I find more information.

- **Go to http://www.google.com/products.** Do an Advanced Product Search using keywords to narrow my search to new hammers, maybe to a certain type and price range, maybe without certain keywords (such as "jackhammer"). Scan the results, clicking on links to Web pages that have more information. I like this better than using a shopping engine, because it finds all hammers sold on the Internet, not just sponsored links.

Check Out the Movers and Shakers

There are usually three or four big companies that produce most of the products in a given market. To identify them, just check the products you research in stores or online; the manufacturer's name is stamped somewhere on the product, packaging, or both. Then go to the websites of those manufacturers and review their product pages or online catalogs. Go to their media page and read any new product releases or articles. Some manufacturers have online stores with retail prices and product descriptions. Some have product pages with wholesale pricing lists.

Other good places to research comparative products and product trends are catalogs, trade magazines, trade organizations, and trade shows. It seems like every trade show has a section with new products, and every trade magazine, industry blog, and trade association website covers new products. Industry experts who lecture and give workshops always talk about where their industry is going.

When you go to a trade show as an observer (rather than as a presenter), your objective is to learn about the industry and to network. Look at all the products. Pay attention to who is manufacturing what, to who the major players are. Go to lectures, and pick up product literature and trade publications. Talk with people. Don't be afraid to ask questions. This is called "walking the show," and it's a good way to meet people, research the market, identify and establish contact with potential licensees, and learn a lot about the industry as a whole very quickly.

Watch and Listen

Many of the top design firms, like IDEO, and even some design schools are advocating "innovation through observation." *Innovation through observation* is observing how people use products at home, at work, or at play to identify their wants, needs, and desires. And it works. Companies routinely come up with new products by observing consumers, conducting focus groups and surveys, and asking the right questions. As previously mentioned, I created the Michael Jordan Wall Ball after just one day of observation.

You can do the same thing. In fact, going shopping to check out comparative products is a form of market observation. But you can go even further with this concept. You can observe people actually using a product similar to yours, watching for ways to improve or enhance it. You can solicit their opinions and ask pointed questions, listening for cues on how to give your idea an added value or a unique sizzle that the other products don't have.

Let's go back to my hypothetical hammer idea. I could go to a construction site and observe carpenters using a hammer. I could go to a friend or a small business owner in my community who builds cabinets or furniture. I could spend a few hours shadowing them as they use a hammer, or better yet, several different hammers. I could ask them what sizes, styles, and name brands of hammers they use; what they like and dislike about each; what's missing; what material their ideal hammer would be made of; and what it would look, feel, and perform like.

When observing, here are some innovation opportunities to watch and listen for:

- Small details that are easy to overlook but equally easy to improve upon
- Flaws or gaps in form or function
- Inefficiencies and inconveniences
- Boring or outdated materials and styles
- Differences in the way different people use or view the product
- Unconventional use of the product

- Other products that people use for the same or a similar purpose
- Potential applications of existing technology

Whether you observe by shopping or by watching and talking with potential consumers of your product, make sure to record your findings. Take notes. Take photos of the products. And take heed of what you've observed. Because, and this is really important, you must be willing and able to adjust your idea to fit the market. Otherwise, consumers won't buy it, and if consumers won't buy it, companies won't license it.

Discover Sleeping Dinosaurs

Finding a sleeping dinosaur simply means finding an opportunity to update or spruce up something that has been around, relatively unchanged, for a long time. It's taking a classic product and breathing new life into it. It's making a small change that packs a big wallop.

For example, when I was at Worlds of Wonder (WOW) in the late 1980s, Paul Rago was the vice president of marketing. Before that, he had been a schoolteacher. Paul came up with ideas by looking at how kids play traditional childhood games and then updating them. One day he decided to take a look at a game kids have been playing forever: tag. "What can we do to update tag?" he asked himself and his team of engineers. "Is there any technology we can apply to tag?" Sure enough, they came up with Lazer Tag, using infrared technology. It was a huge hit and quickly became the top-selling toy for WOW.

Paul Rago applied that same approach to a couple of other things, with amazing results. He looked at all the things kids used in school and created ways to make them fun and fashionable. He looked at the basic backpack and basic duffel bag, really functional items, and said, "Let's make them denim." It was such a simple change that it's amazing no one else had thought of it, especially considering that denim was really popular with kids at the time. Everything was denim—jeans, jackets, shorts, shirts, shoes. Why not bags? It was Paul who asked that question and acted on it. Sack-It became one of the top-selling bags in the world.

He did the same thing with other back-to-school products, creating a whole new product line at WOW called Class Act. Among those designs were cool organizers for lockers and a little recording device for leaving a message for a friend, instead of writing a note and slipping it in his or her locker. Paul brought creativity and technology to a category of products where none had existed before.

Like Paul, you can find those sleeping dinosaurs and revitalize them by making them current. Just look at a product that's been around for a while in a new light. Envision how it would look and work if you jazzed it up or applied new technology to it. Just revamping a sleeping dinosaur a little bit can breathe new life into it, giving consumers an added value and incentive to buy and giving companies a way to boost profits.

Get Creative!

CREATIVITY PLAYS a big role in all aspects of bringing an idea to market. It enables you to come up with novel ideas and to develop those ideas into marketable products. It helps you find fast, easy, inexpensive, and effective ways to prototype your idea. It definitely comes in handy when you're creating your one-line benefit statement and your sell sheet. Your creativity is also an asset when it comes to protecting your idea, figuring out whether it's doable, finding potential licensees, and getting a company to say yes to your idea.

Everyone is creative. Being creative is simply looking at something from a different perspective. It's turning something upside-down and looking at it through a child's eyes, seeing no limitations, seeing only possibilities. Creativity comes naturally to children; they look at the world with wonder and with no boundaries. Everything is new; anything is possible. I remember, as a kid, thinking I could fly and then later, thinking I could build a jet pack, strap it on my back, and fly through the sky.

I believe a streak of childlike creativity is still inside each of us. We don't really lose our creativity as adults. It's just that the weight of the world on our shoulders, all that responsibility we carry around all the time, shoves our creativity into some dark corner inside. But everyone is or can be creative. You just need to tap into that childlike creativity within.

I also believe creativity is a process that anyone can develop. Creativity is about problem solving. It's about wondering how and why, and thinking outside the box. It's about examining what is and asking *what if*. I've found that creativity improves with practice: through constantly looking "differently" at many different things.

I also believe that passion drives creativity and that creativity should be *fun*.

Follow Your Passion

My dad's advice to me when I was trying to figure out what to do with my life—"find what you're passionate about"—makes sense not only for finding your profession, but also for finding design ideas. What better place to look for opportunities to design new and better products than in areas that are of interest or importance to you. I love the toy and novelty and gift markets, and that's where many of my most successful ideas have come from. I was concerned about the lack of information on over-the-counter medication, sometimes with dire consequences, and that led to one of my most successful designs, the Spinformation label.

Maybe you're passionate about child development or the environment. Maybe gardening is your thing, or fishing. Maybe you're a tool nut or a pet lover. Maybe you're into kitchen doodads or electronic gadgets. Whatever turns you on, turn to *that* to find a market or product category for which you might want to design a product.

Is there a store or type of store that you frequent even when you're not buying anything? A catalog you pour over? A hobby or trade magazine you read, including the ads, to find out what's new and interesting? A trade or product show you attend to keep up on the latest and greatest trends? As you go about these normal routines, keep your eyes and mind open for potential markets for your yet-to-be-discovered ideas.

Who knows? Maybe you'll find an idea that combines two things you're passionate about, say, home improvement and the environment, pets and electronics, fishing and child development.

Browse the Mall and Magazines

Oftentimes when I'm looking for a new idea and my creativity seems to be blocked, I will visit the local mall. I'll go into the stores and look at all the merchandise, not only stuff I might be interested in developing or purchasing, but everything. I'll sit in the middle of the mall and watch people shop in the stores. I'll observe what types of products they are purchasing and what products they're drawn to. I'll go into some of the stores and talk with the manager and employees. I'll ask them what's hot and what's not, what trends they are noticing in buying habits. Often they will spill their guts and give me way more information than I needed. Sometimes, they even tell me how their sales have been doing for the last week or month. This type of inside information can be important when developing new products.

That is how I came up with my idea for a fun, interactive cup for kids. I went into the Disney store at my local mall and asked the manager what their most popular product was. He said it was their cups. I saw that some of the plastic cups had a double-layer outer wall. The back layer was a color (red, blue, yellow, etc.), the front layer was clear plastic, and there were sparkles between the two layers. I immediately thought of other images and games you could put between the two layers of plastic, which kids could play by rotating the cup: different dresses for Minnie Mouse; a numbers game with 101 Dalmations; and Sesame Street characters spelling out names. I had actually come up with a similar idea for paper cups a couple of years before, but it was too expensive to manufacture, so I had put it aside. Now I realized the idea could be adapted for plastic cups. I looked on the bottom of the cups in the Disney store and saw the manufacturer's name, Trudeau. They licensed the idea from me, and for five years my rotating character cups were sold in every Disney store and theme park worldwide.

Another place I go to get my creative juices flowing is the bookstore. I go to the magazine aisle, look at all of the trendy entertainment and fashion magazines, and check out what the celebrities are wearing or using. I can spend hours at a time reading those magazines, and sometimes it sparks an idea that's a simple but unique twist on a hot product.

Make a Game of It!

Just sitting at your desk and attempting to pull ideas out of your head is usually not the most effective way of generating a creative idea. Sometimes, you need to feed your brain to stimulate creative thought. There are a number of ways to do that: go shopping, watch a current movie, take a walk, read a magazine, or go to a crowded café and people watch. In fact, making new friends always helps me; they usually have an entirely different perspective. Another way to poke your creativity is to change your habits: take an alternate route to work, listen to a new radio station, read a magazine, or shop at a new store.

When you're in idea-brainstorming mode, don't worry about whether your ideas are good or bad. Don't force or restrict the process. Just let your inhibitions and your mind go. Let the child in you come out. Make a game of it.

The following are three fun games I play to come up with ideas: Mix and Match, What If, and Solve It. Remember, when you play these games, there are no good or bad ideas. You're only playing, just exercising your creativity muscle. If a good idea comes out of it, fantastic. If not, it's still good practice, and you might resurrect that idea one day and reinvigorate it into something even better. If you want to design and license your ideas, you'll need to come up with lots of ideas. So whatever you can do to keep the ideas flowing, do it.

Mix and Match

Pick two different items. Imagine how you might combine these two items to make a completely new product. For example, one of the most popular products right now is the camera phone. Someone simply combined a cell phone with a digital camera. When playing Mix and Match, I recommend combining two products that are normally found together—at least when you're new to this. It's usually much easier to find ways to combine two products used in the kitchen than it is to combine a product used in the kitchen with a product used in the garage.

That said, it is entirely possible to mix and match two products that seemingly have nothing in common, that is, until someone looks at them differently. For example, John Osher's SpinBrush—an electric toothbrush that cost a fraction of what electric toothbrushes at the time cost—was inspired by his Spin Pop, a lollipop that twirls in your mouth when you push a button on the "handle." Toy candy meets dental hygiene. Now, *that's* a winning game of Mix and Match!

What If . . .

This is one of my favorite design games to play. I look at a product and ask, "What if this product did something totally different?" For example, I might look at a hammer and ask, "What if this hammer could hit a nail straight every time?" Or like one of my students, Todd Basche, asked: "What if a combination lock had letters, instead of numbers, so you could spell out your secret code?" He now has a successful product, Wordlock, which is sold in tens of thousands of stores around the world.

Another great example of "what if" (and this has changed an entire industry) is Netflix. In the old days of Hollywood Video and Blockbuster, consumers were charged hefty late fees on their video rentals if they did not return them on time. Someone said "what if there were no late fees?" and Netflix became viable. Now, new companies are asking "what if a consumer could just order a movie from the living room"? You can see the power of the question!

Solve It

For this game, I observe problems that I or other individuals face every day and try to come up with solutions to those problems. For example, after reading an article that stated there is never enough space on product labels to fit all the required and desired information, I solved the problem by inventing Spinformation, which increased the labeling space by 75 percent. The concept is simple: it's two labels, one on top of the other, both held in place with a fixed band. The bottom label is stationary; the top label is a thin plastic film with a clear window on it. The top label spins around the container revealing the information on the base label through the window.

This is the most common way that inventors and product developers come up with ideas. They see a problem in their own lives and try to solve it. You need to be careful, though, because what you think is a problem may not be a problem for everyone, or there may already be a solution to the problem out there that you are unaware of.

Observation is the best way to use this game. By observing and talking to others, you can identify a problem with a broad scope and then come up with a unique solution for it. That way, instead of innovating for yourself, you're innovating for the market, which is the most direct path to licensing your ideas.

PLAYING WITH A $20 MILLION SLEEPING DINOSAUR

If you go to the outdoor water toy aisle of any retailer, you'll see an array of squirt guns of varying sizes, shapes, colors, dimensions, and blasting power. That was not the case 20-some years ago when Lonnie Johnson created the Super Soaker, the first pressurized water gun. At the time, all squirt guns were the same basic, tired design they had been for decades.

Lonnie, a NASA scientist and an inventor by trade, was actually working on a design for a Freon-less heat pump that used water as a working fluid, propelled by jets. When one of the jets accidentally shot a stream of water across the bathroom where he was doing an experiment, he thought, "This would make a great water gun."

Within a year of its debut in 1990, the Super Soaker was the top-selling toy in the United States. And this new twist on an old toy earned Lonnie Johnson about $20 million in royalties.

Lonnie took a sleeping dinosaur and reinvigorated it by playing Mix and Match with a classic water toy and advanced water-jet technology. Of all his inventions, Lonnie ranks the Super Soaker as one of his top three favorites. Not only was it a huge success, it was also a blast!

Coming up with great ideas and bringing them to market can, and should, be fun. If, like Lonnie, you follow your passion and use your creativity during each of the 10 steps outlined in *One Simple Idea*, you'll enjoy the game and win it!

6

Not Creative? Be a Product Scout

COMPANIES IN all industries need ideas. They're desperate for them. Today, a company's success depends on its ability to innovate: to quickly bring new products to market. Few companies can do that solely from ideas they develop in-house. This is where open innovation comes into play.

But many companies don't know how or don't have a system in place to go find those ideas. Likewise, many independent product developers don't know how to license their ideas, and some simply prefer hiring someone to "rep" their ideas to licensees for them.

This scenario creates a huge opportunity for you to profit from connecting innovators with manufacturers. As a product scout, you find great ideas and then find the right companies to license them. In return for your services, the product designer splits the licensing royalty with you. Every time a company sells a product you scouted, you make money.

If you have an entrepreneurial spirit and great selling skills, you can do this. If you have a passion for products, even better! You just need to know how and where to find marketable ideas—and I'll tell you how later in this chapter. First, though, you need to understand these five simple strategies to product-scouting success:

1. Become a licensing expert.
2. Find your niche.
3. Study the market.
4. Focus on ideas you can sell.
5. Cut a win-win agreement.

Become a Licensing Expert

The main reason independent product designers hire product scouts is because they don't have the expertise to license their ideas to companies themselves. Some product designers choose to work with a licensing expert because they want to focus on creating ideas rather than selling them. In either case, they'll expect *you* to be the licensing expertise. After all, that's what they're paying you for. The more you know, the more successful you'll be.

As a product scout, your success depends on three things:

- How many of the ideas you scout out *get licensed*
- How many of those licensed ideas *get to market*
- How *well those ideas sell* on the market

So it is vitally important for you to become a licensing expert: a master at finding marketable ideas and getting them into the marketplace. That's the only way you're going to be able to convince designers to let you pitch their ideas to companies, and that's the only way you're going to be able to convince companies to bring those ideas to market.

You can acquire licensing knowledge from various sources: books, classes, seminars, trade associations, mentors, and groups such as LES—Licensing Executives Society, which comprises nearly 5,000 members engaged in the transfer, use, development, manufacture, and marketing of intellectual property. For example, at inventRight we offer courses with CDs and workbooks as well as online classes and other tools for learning how to find, develop, and license great ideas. Another great resource is Ideapow: an "online learning lab" for "entrepreneurial-minded people" who want to learn how to license ideas to companies. Ideapow's step-by-step instructional program also includes a directory of more than 1,300 companies looking for ideas.

Wherever you turn for information and training on licensing ideas, just make sure that the information comes from a licensing expert—someone with firsthand experience in licensing products. Of course, the only way to get your *own* experience is to find marketable ideas and then find companies to license them. The more products you license, the more credibility you'll have with both designers and manufacturers.

Find Your Niche

To scout ideas, you can take either the shotgun approach or the high-powered rifle approach. You can shoot out your feelers here, there, and everywhere until you strike something big. Or you can narrow your search to a specific industry, market, or even product category and zero in on a simple idea with mega market potential. My advice, especially when you're first starting out, is to take the rifle approach and focus on an industry you're familiar with, a market you're interested in, or a product category you're passionate about.

Find your market niche and look there for ideas first. Generally speaking, this is a more efficient, productive, and profitable use of your time and talents. It increases your chances of finding good ideas and getting them licensed. It takes less time to scout, research, and network in one or two industries than in three, four, or more. At least some of the work you do for one idea will be useful for other ideas. Success builds on success. For example, if three or four of your clients have big hits in the novelty and gift industry, it will be easier for you to secure other novelty and gift designers as clients and to get novelty and gift companies to open their doors to you.

That does not mean you need to, or even should, limit yourself to one market. Feel free to go scouting wherever you might find good ideas that interest you. It's just easier to get started when you narrow your search.

Identify Hot Markets

Study the marketplace, as discussed in Chapter 4, to find industries and product categories with strong sales and growth potential. Check out TV shopping channels, consumer magazines, mail-order catalogs, online shopping portals, big-box retailers, and specialty retailers to identify robust and emerging markets as well as product trends. For example, pets, kitchen gadgets, home improvement, and "staycation" product categories are hot at the time of this writing. Other industries and product categories might be heating up as you read this. Still others might be coming down the pike. Markets change constantly and quickly, and it is imperative to stay plugged into new and emerging trends.

Once you've identified hot industries and product categories that you're interested in, study those markets to learn everything you can about them. The more familiar you are with a market, the easier it will be for you to find ideas and the more likely you'll be to recognize a marketable idea. Studying a specific market will also increase your likelihood of finding one great idea after another, which is critical to your continued success as a product scout.

This does not mean you need to be an expert in every industry you want to work in. You just need to know the market well enough to make good judgments about an idea's market potential. To familiarize yourself with a market, you can do the same things that designers and inventors do, or should do, before they design a product: Go shopping. Talk to retailers and consumers. Search the Internet. Read trade publications. Go to trade shows. Check out the websites of trade associations and major manufacturers in that market.

Focus on Ideas You Can License

Be selective in choosing which ideas to take on. Just because an idea is clever doesn't mean it will sell. If an idea is too much of a departure from other products in the market or if the technology is too new or complicated, you could invest a lot of your time and hard work for nothing—only to discover that no company wants to license it. Taking on an idea that you have doubts about or that you don't have good reason to believe can be manufactured and sold is a waste of your time and only gives false hope to the designer or inventor.

That does not mean you should limit yourself to only ideas with big markets and a huge profit potential. In fact, I think that's a bad strategy, because those hot ideas tend to be few and far between. To be a successful product scout and to maximize your income, you need to find as many marketable ideas as possible and get them to market as quickly and easily as possible. Often, a simple idea—a small change to an existing product—can be a slam dunk to license. Sometimes you can hit a home run with a new twist on an old idea. Just make sure the time you spend on an idea is commensurate with its profit potential.

I've found that some designers can talk for a long time but still not give a clear vision of what their idea is. Sometimes, the idea simply isn't ready yet, and the product developer has more homework and legwork to do. To maximize the return on your time, you need to manage the process and get the inventor working for you. That's why it's important to evaluate an idea *before* you agree to take it on and to control the process every step of the way.

First, you should let the designers know upfront that you only take on ideas you think you can license. Tell them that to make that determination, you need for them to provide you with certain information before you can discuss their idea with them. Then use a checklist or submission form that specifies the information you need to evaluate the idea. At the minimum, designers should provide you with these four items:

1. A brief description of their idea, stating its features and benefits. Ask them to limit this *benefit statement* to one or two sentences. Give them a couple examples, such as "I have a five-dollar ballpoint pen that writes at any angle, including upside-down, and writes as smoothly as similar pens that retail for five to ten times more," and "I have a lightweight hammer that hits nails straight every time."
2. A drawing or a computer model of their idea, or a photograph of a prototype of their idea.
3. A list of stores, catalogs, or websites that might sell their product.
4. Applied for intellectual property. (See Chapter 11.)

Some designers will balk at sharing this information. Just explain why you need it and assure them you will hold it in strict confidence. If they provide the information, move forward with the evaluation process. If they don't, let it go. This will help you pick out designers who are serious about getting their ideas licensed and willing to go the whole nine yards with you. In fact, you will probably need more information while you assess the idea. Again, be very specific. The designer's responses will help you determine whether the idea is ready to be licensed and how much work you'll need to do to license it.

Get It in Writing

Once you and a designer decide to work together, you'll need an agreement that authorizes you to present his or her idea to potential licensees and spells out the terms and conditions of the agreement, including your compensation.

These are legally binding documents, and every situation is different. So I strongly recommend that you consult with a legal professional for all contracts. But here are some things to consider:

- Plan on sharing any advances and royalties with the designer. You can start by asking for a fifty-fifty split on royalty income. It is their idea, but you will have done a lot of work to license it. You both deserve to be compensated.
- From the client's perspective, the ideal agreement includes a clause that essentially says you'll work for free for a specific period of time, three or six months, and you'll only be compensated if you are successful in licensing the idea within that time frame. If you license the idea, you'll receive a specified share of royalties; if you don't license the idea by the time the contract expires, the designer owes you nothing.
- Entering into an "exclusive" agreement ensures that no one else—including the product developer—can license the idea to a company during the time your contract is in force. This prevents someone else from competing with you.

- No designer or inventor wants to share or relinquish any ownership rights to their idea. So the agreement should specify that the designer owns all rights to the idea. Should you make any improvements to the idea, you should assign all such improvements to the designer. This is the ethical thing to do and will guard your integrity.

- Let's say you are unable to license the idea during the length of the contract, but a few days or weeks or months later, one of the companies you were wooing decides to license the idea. It often takes time for companies to evaluate and make a decision on an idea. It also takes a lot of your time and work to make that happen. So it's a good idea to include a provision in your agreement that allows you to retain the right to license to any of the companies that you contacted during the length of the contract for a certain period of time after the contract expires. For example, if your initial contract is for six months, you should retain the right to license to companies you contacted during that time for at least another three or four months.

Where to Find Marketable Ideas

Ideas are everywhere, literally. In the United States alone, about 180,000 patents are filed every year, and there are thousands of other great ideas out there for which patents have not yet been filed. Listing all the potential places for you to look for ideas is impossible here; the list is just too long. But the following are some of the best ways to find product developers and scout products.

"Shop" the Internet

Many designers think they can simply list their ideas on a website and it will somehow sell itself. Companies simply do not search these sites for ideas. But you can, and you know how to evaluate an idea. These designers are likely to be desperate for some help licensing their ideas.

Try typing these keywords into your browser and then bookmark any sites that you like:

- "Invention for sale" or "inventions for sale"
- "Patent for sale" or "patents for sale"
- "Invention listing sites"

Visit Inventor Forums

Do an Internet search for "inventors forums" or "inventors discussion groups" to find forums where you can go check out what's on the minds and drawing boards of designers. At first, just read the posts, which you can do for free at most sites, though you'll need to register. If you want to participate in forum discussions, you may need to pay a fee. Use a signature that doesn't scream "product scout." Always offer helpful advice and keep your posts brief. Spending time in forums will give you great insight into the minds of independent designers, and you may find some whom you'll want to talk with privately.

Discover New Patents

Where there are recently issued patents, there are excited designers eager to license their ideas. All industrial nations have patent or intellectual property departments, and most of those have websites where you can do patent searches. Here is the URL for the U.S. Patent Office (USPTO): http://www.uspto.gov/index.html. You can also search for new patents at the website of the World Intellectual Property Organization (WIPO): http://www.wipo.org. Other resources as well as links to the U.K. and Canadian Patent Offices can be found in the Appendix.

Network with Trade Associations

In the United States, there are national trade associations as well as state and regional associations catering to inventors, industrial designers, and various engineering disciplines. Other countries have similar types of associations, and there are several international organizations of this type. Serious inventors and independent designers are often active participants in these organizations, so it's a good way to meet them, learn from them, and find great ideas to license. These are too numerous and diverse to list here, but they're easy enough to find by using the right keywords.

Mine the Talent at Art and Design Schools

These schools are where some of the most creative people around learn how to bring their ideas to life. If I were a product scout, this is the first place I would look for innovative ideas and creative talent. Art and design schools are a gold mine of great ideas.

Not long ago, I was asked to speak at the Art Center College of Design in Pasadena, California. There are schools like Art Center College across the United States, and they are the premier design schools in the country. The Art Center College of Design teaches in 12 different disciplines—everything from industrial design, packaging, and graphic design to website development, transportation design, and more. Students pay up to $200,000 to go to these schools, and those students are the cream of the crop.

Mateo Neri, an instructor at the school in Pasadena, teaches students how to bring a product to market the old way, by starting a business. Mateo found me and asked me to speak to his classes because he discovered that the students did not want to start companies in order to bring their ideas to market. He realized they needed help in licensing their idea.

When I went to the school to speak, I was blown away when I saw their gallery of ideas. They were some of the most innovative and creative ideas and products I had ever seen. Mateo told me that all of those prototypes, drawings, and ideas were all thrown away at the end of the semester. I was heartbroken. I saw such potential in many of the ideas. I knew we had to do something to help these students. So Mateo and I are working together to develop a website called Ideapow, where these creative students, alumni, and others can learn about licensing their ideas and making money from their creativity.

Connect with Research Universities

Many public and private universities that do research routinely license new technology they have developed. These schools account for more than 4,000 new patents and more than 3,500 new licensing agreements per year. Over 60 percent of licenses granted by these universities go to businesses of 500 or fewer employers, and one-third of new innovations created by research universities get licensed. This creates a great opportunity for you to help them license their new innovations. Make yourself known to these universities, and network with program directors and educators in your areas of interest. There are more than 100 public research universities and 50 private research universities in the United States alone. You can find 61 of the 106 U.S. public research universities at http://www.aau.edu.

Publicize Your Services and Achievements

You should publicize constantly, not only when you first launch your business. Every time you license a product for a client, add a new service, extend your services to a new market or industry, have an upcoming speaking engagement, or any other "newsworthy" event, publicize it. Many people think publicity means placing an ad somewhere. Though advertising in magazines, newsletters, online classifieds, special member websites, and other venues can bring ideas to you, it can also be pricey. So if you go that route, always try to negotiate a better rate.

Here are other ways to get "free publicity" to help you to find marketable ideas:

- **Business card and e-mail signature.** These are your calling cards. Maximize their public relations (PR) potential by ensuring they look professional, clearly stating what you do (e.g., "Licensing Expert" or "President/Innovation Licensing, LTD"), and including a *tagline* that succinctly states the gist of your business (e.g., "Helping You License Your Ideas!").

- **Articles and guest blogs.** Writing informative pieces on licensing and interviews or profiles of product designers and inventors for magazines, newsletters, websites, and so on gives you great exposure and credibility.
- **Events and lectures.** Offer lectures to trade associations and groups, and host events, either on-site or online, that introduce you and your services to potential clients and help establish you as an expert in the field.
- **Network with associations.** Join and participate in, or at least make yourself known to, whichever associations, organizations, and groups cater to people who dream up ideas for products in your areas of interest.
- **Network with business advisors.** Few business advisors understand licensing. If they are aware of your services and you've established a working relationship with them, whenever they get a client who needs help licensing their idea, they're likely to refer them to you.
- **Newsletter.** Create a free e-mail or printed newsletter to send to current and potential clients. Send it no more than twice a month and no less than every other month, so as to keep you in their mind without annoying them. Include plenty of helpful information, not just marketing hype.
- **Trade shows.** Attend trade shows not only for inventors and product designers but also for the industries in which you're licensing products. "Walk the show," and network with both attendees and vendors. If you have a number of clients in the same industry, you may want to consider renting a booth and charging each client a percentage of the cost.
- **Website.** Make sure your site is professional-looking, clearly states what you do, establishes you as a licensing expert, and invites people to hire you to find a licensee for their ideas. Update the site frequently, announcing every new service, event, and success.

Finding marketable ideas is the first and most important step to becoming a successful product scout. Keep in mind that the most marketable ideas are often simple ideas: small improvements or enhancements to an existing product, process, or technology.

Of course, becoming a successful product scout involves more than finding marketable ideas. That's why I offer courses, information, and coaching specifically for product scouts. Plus, every chapter in this book pertains to product scouting and will bring you that much closer to creating the life of your dreams by connecting innovators with manufacturers and bringing other people's ideas to market.

How Warren Helps Bring Other People's Ideas to Market

For 20 years, Warren Tuttle worked in the housewares industry, first as a buyer for a major New York City department store, next as the designer of his own line of gourmet cookware that sold in food stores, and then as the owner of an upscale housewares store. About 12 years ago, Warren decided he wanted to bring not only his own but also other people's innovative houseware ideas to market. In his first five years as a product scout, the products Warren was responsible for brought in more than $300 million in sales.

A few years ago, Warren partnered up with Lifetime Brands (LB) to bring in product ideas from outside the company. At the time, LB had an internal research and development (R&D) team of 40 people, and the external product development program was the first of its kind. In less than two years, Warren has brokered 21 licensing deals between LB and independent product developers. He also continues to develop and license his own ideas.

Warren attributes his licensing success to his extensive knowledge and experience in the housewares industry, which he says has given him the "ability to assess new ideas." He also studies the market, keeps abreast of what's going on in the industry as a whole, and maintains a high profile with product developers and inventors. Some of his connections date back 20 to 30 years, and he's always networking and scouting new ideas. Consequently, people constantly refer inventors and product developers to him, to the tune of 1,200 to 1,500 leads a year.

Because of his market expertise, Warren Tuttle knows a winner when he scouts one, and that has resulted in licensing royalties for both Warren and the people whose ideas he has helped bring to market.

To play this game, you don't need to be a creative genius. You don't even need to come up with your own ideas; you can play—and win— by connecting people with great ideas to the companies that want to license them. If you have a passion for innovative products, a penchant for selling, and some licensing expertise, you, too, can reap the rewards of the licensing lifestyle by becoming a product scout.

7

How to Pick Winners

OK, YOU'VE followed your passion, studied the market, poked some sleeping dinosaurs, identified a few hot markets, and brainstormed a slew of intriguing ideas that are buzzing around in your head like a swarm of bees. Now you need to hone in on the best ideas. Then narrow your focus even more and pick one simple idea to work on—the one that lights a fire in your belly because your research and gut tells you it's a winner.

The Four Characteristics of a Winning Idea

You're going to have a lot of ideas, and you need to be able to quickly distinguish between the winners and the losers. I still get lots of ideas and I love all of them! But I'm very selective about which ones I pursue. I only work on potential winners, and I make that determination quickly.

If you want to be successful at this, you, too, need to be able to quickly assess an idea to determine whether it's worth moving forward with, before you say, "OK, now I'm going to work on this." At the end of the day, it's not about how big or small, how complex or simple, or how unique or clever your idea is. It's about which idea is going to take the least amount of work *and* has the highest probability of success.

Many people struggle with this. They come up with a bunch of ideas, and they can't decide which one to work on first or they try to work on several at the same time. You can't work on all 10 of your ideas at once! It is usually more productive to focus on one idea at a time.

I also recommend starting with a simple idea and taking it all the way through the whole development and licensing process. It's just so much easier and faster to bring an idea to market that is an enhancement, improvement, or unique takeoff on a proven product. Once you've done this, you'll be more confident, knowledgeable, and efficient with your next idea. As you get some successes under your belt, you'll get better and faster at zeroing in on whether an idea is marketable and on how to design it to fit the market.

So especially in the beginning, stick with simple ideas in a proven market. Bigger and more complicated ideas can take a while and present you with some real challenges. You don't want your first few ideas to hang you up. That will just discourage and frustrate you. You want to get going, get through all the steps, and get your ideas in front of the right people and into the marketplace, so you can start collecting royalties.

Whenever I come up with an idea I'm interested in, I give it this four-step litmus test to see if it's a potential winner worth pursuing further:

1. Does it solve a common problem?
2. Does it have a wow factor?
3. Does it have a large market?
4. Does it use common production methods and materials?

Does It Solve a Common Problem?

The idea with the best chance of success is the one that virtually anyone can look at and immediately know how it solves an everyday problem, satisfies a prevalent need or want, or fills an obvious void in the market. As a rule of thumb, the more universal the problem and your solution, the easier it is to license it.

Companies don't want to educate the market about a product or create a new market for a product. They're like me: they like ideas that are simple to explain and easy to show its unique value. They want ideas that consumers will take one look at and say, "I get it. I love it! I see how it benefits me. I want it."

Don't assume there's a need for your idea or base this determination on guesswork. Study the market and do whatever homework you need to determine whether your idea solves a common problem. Confirmed and well-defined needs are a lot easier to license than maybes.

Does It Have a Wow Factor?

How does your idea stack up against the competition? Is it going to stand out in the crowd? Does it have one clear and exciting benefit that other comparable products don't and that consumers want? A small change to an existing product is often the most marketable, but it has to sizzle. It has to grab the attention of potential buyers and make them want to open their wallets. It has to wow potential licensees, dazzling them with some outstanding feature they know will give them a competitive edge and making them want to license your idea.

Again, don't just assume that the market is as crazy about your idea as you are. Do some comparison shopping, talk with store clerks, observe customers, and verify that your idea has a wow factor that sets it apart from the competition.

Does It Have a Large Market?

When I develop a product, I want all the major retailers for that product category to sell it and I want them to sell a lot of it, because an idea with that kind of potential market really motivates potential licensees. Sometimes I work on ideas with a smaller market, but only if I think I can find a licensee for it relatively quickly and easily. Often, it takes as much time and work to license a big-market idea as it does to license an idea with a moderate-sized market. It just makes sense to put most of your time where the most money is.

So before you decide to move forward with an idea, you should find out whether the potential market for your idea is big enough. Let's say you have an idea for an iPad wine-guide application. For starters, you're in a growth product category. The market for iPad applications is huge right now. But how big is the market for electronic mobile wine guides? Well, to gauge the size of that market, you'd need to find out how many people buy wine and how many wine buyers are likely to have or purchase iPads. My gut and my initial market observation indicate it's a sizable market, but if it were my idea, I'd still do some basic market research to verify and quantify the size of the market.

It's easy to estimate the size of the potential market for your idea: just study the market. Find out whether the product category is a growth category, whether comparable products are selling well, and how they're priced. Get a profile of the industry or product category, detailing what is selling, who is buying, what they're paying, whether sales are increasing or declining, who the major players are, any up and coming trends, and so on. You can find this information through search engines, shopping, industry experts, trade associations, trade magazines (media kits often include industry profiles), marketing think tanks, and other resources.

Does It Use Common Production Methods and Materials?

Once you've piqued a potential licensee's interest in your idea, the first two questions the licensee will ask are, "How will it be manufactured?" and "How much will that cost?" In Chapter 9 you'll learn how to find and give the right answers to those two critical questions. But for now, to decide whether to even work on the idea, you need to get a feel for how doable and affordable it is to produce. That's easy enough to find out. If your idea can be manufactured using technology, materials, manufacturing equipment, and production processes that already exist, then it's definitely doable. If those methods and materials are already being used widely in your product category, then your idea is probably affordable—and profitable—for a potential licensee to produce.

Again, this is where your market research really pays off. What helps even more, supplementing your own findings, is to cultivate a network of industry experts that you can call on. Among your network, you may even find a mentor to help guide you through difficult dealings.

Find Someone Who Has Done It Before

My father used to say, "Whatever you do in life, find someone who has already done it, get as close as you can, and learn as much as you can." I didn't know it then, but that was great advice. And it's one of the best pieces of advice I can give to anyone who wants to license his or her ideas.

So many people try to do this on their own, with no input from an insider who really knows the market. Frankly, I think that's crazy. I've been developing and licensing products, and I can't tell you how often I'll be working on a new idea and very quickly realize that I don't have all the information. So my first step is always to study the market. And my next is to find experts in that field and pick their brains.

If your idea is a gag gift, find someone who designs, makes, or sells novelty items or who has firsthand knowledge of that industry, such as a trade magazine editor or a trade association leader. If your idea is a kitchen gadget, find an expert in that product category. If your idea is a cool twist on a punching bag, find a leader in the sporting goods industry. Find out who the major players are and what they have to say about what's going on in the market. Read trade magazines. Visit the websites of the top designers and manufacturers in the field. Go to trade shows where they are presenting, sit in on their lectures, and talk with them.

Talk with them? Yes, talk with them. I realize that asking a stranger for help can seem intimidating, even impossible. But it is possible. There *is* someone out there who is willing and able to give you advice and information. Many people who have achieved success are glad to share what they've learned. They're in a position to help, and they want to help others succeed, too. Some pros are even willing to take on a protégé, to be your mentor—to show you the ropes. A knowledgeable and accessible mentor will be invaluable in helping you assess the viability of your idea and then develop it for the market.

You just need to find these experts and ask for the help you need. The worst that can happen is someone will say no. Then you just keep looking until you find someone else who is ready, willing, and able to give back.

How to Find a Pro

To find a pro who might be able and willing to answer my questions, I often go online and search for an expert in that field. For example, if I were working on a health care product, I would look for someone who has written an article, given a seminar, or been a speaker at a trade show or conference geared toward the health care products industry. I might call the editor of a trade magazine or a trade association and ask for the name of someone who really knows whatever product category I'm working in. I might go to a trade show and look for someone to network with there.

Often, I find someone who has done something similar, give that person a call, and say straight up, "I'm working on this project, and I have a question I'd like to ask you." I stroke the person's ego a little— compliment the person on his or her successful products, acknowledge the person's expertise, and ask the person a question that's right up his or her alley. I always find someone who is willing, able, and qualified to give me the information, advice, or opinion I need or to at least direct me to someone else who might.

Go for the Gold

When seeking out mentors and industry experts to learn from, make sure their expertise is relevant to your idea. Be wary of information that comes from someone who does not have experience in the industry or product category you need. The person best able to help you along your journey is someone who has done it before, who has had success developing and licensing products in the same field as your idea.

Nothing beats having a two-way dialogue with a real person who has walked the walk. I think this is so important, because in anything you do, there are always twists and turns. Questions come up. Challenges arise. So do opportunities. It is so helpful to be able to ask someone who knows the ropes, "Hey, what do you think? . . . What should I look out for? . . . What do I need to know? . . . Who might be interested in licensing my idea?" And sometimes, it just helps to "talk shop" with someone who's walking the same path that you're on.

How My Mentor Changed My Life

I was fortunate to meet the man who would become my mentor when I was in my early 20s and first starting out as a product designer. One day someone came up to my booth at the Sausalito Art Festival and said, "Your products should be everywhere, and I know just the guy who can do that for you. His name is Stephen Askin. He has a showroom in Los Angeles called What's New."

So I called and asked to speak with Stephen Askin. Sixty seconds later, he was on the line. I told him the name of my company was Softees, and he needed to see my products. He said, "Sure. Come on down." I made the six-hour drive to L.A. with my father. When I walked into the showroom, my heart thumped wildly in my chest. It was filled with soft sculpted toys and novelty items.

Stephen Askin represented artists from across the United States. That day they were getting ready for their big trade show, which drew retailers from across the country. Stephen nodded toward my boxes and said, "Let's see." When I started pulling out my hand-crafted sculpted animals and characters, his eyes lit up. He told me he loved them, and he told his staff to put them in the showroom for retailers to order. An hour later, I was in his office signing a contract.

Dad and I sat in funny chairs that had feet for legs, one wearing cowboy boots, the other tennis shoes. Stephen Askin sat across the desk from us wearing funny eye glasses and a Deely Bobbers hat that bobbed dollar signs in front of his face. Everywhere we looked, we saw toys. My father, a tenured executive at General Electric, was shocked. I felt right at home. I had also found someone who believed in me and my products.

It was one of the best days of my life, and it changed my life forever. Stephen Askin took a chance on me. He took my phone call, he gave me a big break, and he advised me every step of the way.

Later, when I couldn't keep up with all the orders that were coming in from retailers across the country, he stepped up to the plate again. "Teach my workers how to make your products using our equipment, rather than by hand. Then we'll take care of the manufacturing and distribution for you." Looking back, I guess that was my first licensing deal.

Among the many things I learned from Stephen Askin over the 30 years he's been my mentor is the importance of designing a product so that it can be produced at the right price point so that it can retail for the right price point. Today, with more than 20 licensed products under my belt, I still run ideas by Stephen Askin. We still talk on the phone every week or whenever I need some advice from my favorite mentor. He still works in an office filled with toys and novelties. And he still wears funny glasses and Deely Bobbers.

Although it wasn't exactly what my father had in mind, Dad was spot on: Find someone who is doing exactly what you want to do, and learn from him or her. Find a mentor!

Become an Expert in Any Field in 24 Hours or Less

When you're looking at all the ideas you've brainstormed trying to figure out which ones to pursue, it's not enough to ask an industry expert what he or she thinks. In fact, some industry experts wouldn't recognize a good idea if it walked up to them, introduced itself, and had "million-dollar idea" written all over it. Sometimes, because you're *not* an expert in a field, you can look at things differently and see simple ideas with mega marketing potential that the "experts" might overlook. But once you get an idea that fires you up, you need to gain some expertise in that field so you can make good decisions about whether and how to move forward with it.

What you need is a clear snapshot of the playing field. What are the hot products in the market now? What are their features, benefits, and price points? How are they packaged and displayed? Which companies manufacture them? Where are they sold? How well are they selling? Who is buying them? How are sales industrywide or for that product category? What are the emerging trends in the field?

All of this information can be obtained by studying the market, using all of the techniques discussed in Chapter 4.

Trust Your Gut

People ask me all the time, "Stephen, what do you think of my idea?" If I know the market, I'll give my opinion. But it's just that: an opinion.

Now, there are consultants out there who charge people to evaluate their ideas. I believe that's nonsense. For one thing, the only opinions that really matter are the opinions of potential licensees. And if you do this right, you've thoroughly evaluated the idea yourself (which is what Chapters 4 through 10 of this book are all about), plus you've gotten *free* advice from someone who has successfully done what you're trying to do. So beyond that, you just need to trust your gut.

One thing almost all product developers do, myself included, is run their ideas by family and friends. And that's fine. Just make sure to take their opinions with a grain of salt and not to heart. They are consumers, after all, so their opinions may well have merit. But they do not have industry expertise. Even if they are familiar with an industry or product category, they haven't done the research you've done on your idea. So hear them out, but trust your research and your gut.

I learned the importance of this several years ago with one of my early ideas. Every night, after we had put the kids to bed, my wife and I would slip into bed and I'd bring out my big sketch pad and show her my ideas. It was a fun time for us to talk and laugh—and Janice always laughed at my bad ideas. I would always start with the worst idea and save the best for last. Well, one night after showing her and laughing with her about my bad ideas, I brought out the best idea I had come up with that day. I had spent several hours researching, thinking about, and tinkering with the idea. I had even made a crude prototype: it was the Michael Jordan Wall Ball that I discussed earlier in this book. I made it with cardboard, a photocopy of a poster of Michael Jordan I had bought for five dollars or so, and some tape.

So I showed it to Janice, fully expecting her to tell me what a great idea it was. Instead, Janice looked at me and said, and I quote, "Steve, the chances of you licensing this idea are one in a million. Forget about it, go do something else." Ouch!

Janice is one of the smartest people I know. She went to Stanford University and has an MBA from The Kellogg School of Management at Northwestern. She has had an impressive career in marketing and product development, and even has experience in the toy industry. In fact, I met her at Worlds of Wonder, where she brought to market the company's biggest-selling toy ever, Lazer Tag. Before that, she was at Clorox, and she went on to be the vice president of marketing at E&J Gallo Winery, one of the highest-ranking women in the company's history. So I respect her opinion very much, and I was crushed for a few minutes there.

But I had done my market research. I had gone to Toys "R" Us and saw that all the indoor basketball backboards were square and boring. I noticed one with a small photo of Michael Jordan on it, from Ohio Art, so I knew they had the Michael Jordan license, but the picture was really small. I'm a basketball player, and I know the toy industry. *This is terrible,* I thought. *Michael needs to be bigger. This needs better graphics. It needs to be more exciting.* I knew it could be manufactured at the right price point. I just *knew* I had something.

So the very next day I sent off my idea to Ohio Art. In fact, I believed so strongly in my idea that I sent it by next-day delivery service. Three days later, Ohio Art put a licensing contract in the mail to me.

Soon, it was on store shelves everywhere, including the coveted end-cap display at Walmart. It was on the front of the Wheaties box as a premium. One Saturday morning, my wife and I were sitting in front of the TV watching cartoons with our three kids, and the Michael Jordan Wall Ball commercial came on. As Michael Jordan looked into the camera and said, "This is the best-looking backboard I've ever seen," I looked over at Janice, smiled, and gave her a little I-told-you-so look.

An idea my brilliant and knowledgeable wife said had a one-in-a-million chance of getting licensed—an idea that took me less than a day to come up with, about 15 minutes to prototype and send out, and about a week to license—ended up selling for ten years and earning me more than $250,000 in royalties.

So be careful about the input you get from other people, even people whose opinions you value.

At the end of the day, if you've done your market research and if your idea passes the four-point litmus test, you can trust your gut that you have a potential winner. But before you put your idea to the ultimate test—submitting it to a potential licensee—there are a few simple things you should do to prove and protect your idea, as you'll learn about in Chapters 8 to 12.

PART THREE

Prove Your Idea

You've come up with an idea you're passionate about. Your market research has convinced you the idea has the markings of a winner. Now you're eager to get it developed, get it to market, and start getting royalties!

Whoa! Hold on a minute.

Have you done the research, analysis, and design work needed to prove your idea will sell? To prove your idea is doable? To prove it can be sold at a price and made at a cost that is profitable?

Before you pour your blood, sweat, and tears as well as a lot of time and resources into building a fancy prototype, patenting your idea, and trying to find licensees, you should evaluate your idea and do a little more homework, so you can give the right answers to those deal-making, or deal-breaking, questions.

Will It Sell?

T HE CONVENTIONAL method of developing and licensing a product goes something like this: You come up with an idea and sketch it out. You spend six months to a year and thousands, if not tens of thousands, of dollars building a prototype, during which you run into all kinds of problems and repeatedly go back to the drawing board to iron out the kinks, fix the prototype, or build a new one, until you get it right. You file a patent application, which costs thousands of dollars and takes days, weeks, or months to do, depending on how much patent research and how many design adjustments you need to do. Once the design meets your satisfaction and the patent is filed, you wait three or four years until the patent is issued. By then, five to six years have gone by and you're wondering, "Now what do I do?"

Twenty years ago or so, I looked at that scenario and said to myself, "That's all wrong. That is not for me." I knew I wanted to make a career out of coming up with ideas, out of being creative. I wanted to see my ideas on the store shelf. That was my goal. But if I had to spend more than $10,000 every time I had an idea? Well, there was no way I would fulfill that goal. My wife would never allow it! You see, I knew that inventing was a numbers game.

When I worked at Worlds of Wonder, we were often presented with 20 or more ideas at a time to consider—hundreds of ideas every year—and only a handful actually became products that were sold in retail. Why? More often than not, it was because the idea didn't hit all the market targets. It wasn't unique enough. It was too far removed from the norm. It didn't have a wow factor. It wasn't the right price point. It didn't have a big enough market. It wasn't what the market needed, wanted, or could afford. Bottom line: it wouldn't sell.

I learned the importance of answering the question "Will it sell?" early in my career. During the seven years I spent designing stuffed animals and characters and selling them on street corners and at state fairs, county fairs, crafts fairs, wherever I could set up a table, I found out very quickly that if a product didn't sell, I didn't eat. So I would always test the market before bringing out anything new. I'd make a small number of the new product, and if people immediately started looking at it, asking questions about it, and buying it, I could tell within a few days if it was going to sell and how well it would sell.

Later, when I set up shop as an independent product developer, I didn't want to spend a lot of money, time, and effort developing an idea only to be told no. To get potential licensees to say yes, I needed to know that my idea would sell before I presented it to them. Actually, I decided I needed to know whether my idea would sell before I went to the trouble of developing it.

That's when I realized that I needed to design *for* the market, rather than design something and then test the market. At the same time, I decided I wanted to be able to sell potential licensees my ideas without having to build fancy prototypes and get expensive patents. What I came up with are a few simple strategies for quickly and cost-effectively proving that an idea will sell and can be brought to market easily and profitably. I've had a lot of success with these strategies and so have many of my students. You can too.

I've touched on the first and most important strategy already, which is to design *for* the market. To do that, you have to assess the market-ability of your idea, tweak your idea accordingly, and then define your market so you can prove to potential licensees that your idea will sell.

Innovate for the Market

Through the homework you did to come up with a great idea to work on (Chapters 4 to 7), you got a sense for the size of your market and where your idea fits into it. In the process, you may even have tweaked your idea a bit based on what you learned. Now the real product development work begins. Now it's time to look again at the market and at your idea—closely, objectively, and honestly—and then innovate for it.

Innovating for the market is actually a step up from designing for the market. Innovating means coming up with something truly new and exciting, something nobody else is doing, and something with a far-reaching benefit and a definite wow factor. The cool thing is that you don't need to reinvent the wheel or introduce a revolutionary new concept or technology to innovate. You can take a simple idea, look at it differently, and give it an innovative new twist that will blow consumers away! Those are the kinds of ideas companies are begging for. And those are the kinds of ideas you and I are well equipped to come up with, because we *are* the consumers, and we know what we like and what we don't like.

Study the market. Compare and contrast your idea with similar products out there. How is it similar and different? Look at other products in your category and at other product categories that consumers of your product also favor. Check out both the low-end and high-end of the market, as well as all the points in between. What's missing? Where are the holes? What hasn't been done before? What two products or technologies could be combined to make a better product? What new and emerging market trends have yet to be applied or combined in your product category?

Pay attention to details; that's where you'll usually find the most opportunities for simple changes that have big impacts. Sit back and look at your idea with fresh eyes, searching for and envisioning ways to shape and refine the design to maximize its marketability. Are there ways to improve its form, functionality, or both? To broaden its appeal? To fill holes in the market? To make it sizzle? Let your mind wander and keep an open mind; if something pops into your mind, write it down. Explore it. Consider all possibilities.

Write everything down, all your research notes and design ideas. When you're shopping, take photographs of design elements you might want to "borrow" from. Print photos you find on the Internet.

Sketch out the different permutations of your idea, or do what I some-times do and cut and paste together images and photographs from magazines, product packaging, sales literature, and so on.

Remember, if an element of your design exists somewhere in the marketplace, in one product category or another, it's probably doable for your idea, that is, a potential licensee can probably manufacture your product at a profitable cost. When a company is interested in licensing your idea, two of the most important questions they'll ask are, "How do we make it?" and "How much will it cost?" Chapter 9 tells you how to find the answers to those questions. But for this step of the process—when you're creating and developing your idea—you only need to determine that it is probably doable. The main focus now is to figure out how to give your idea a wow factor that will catch the attention of potential licensees.

Take, for example, a simple idea for unclogging household drains that my inventRight student Gene Luoma came up with. Everyone has sink, shower, or tub drains in their homes, and every drain gets clogged at one time or another. Gene studied products for unclogging drains on the market and came up with a better solution to this com-mon problem.

He observed that when a drain gets clogged, most people reach for a plunger. When that doesn't work, they pour in liquid or crystal drain cleaners, which don't always work and, as Gene noted, are both expensive and toxic. He learned that some people try to unclog drains with a coat hanger, which rarely works, or with a plumber's snake, which only works if you know what you're doing (if you don't, you can damage the plumbing). As a last resort, he learned, people just call in a plumber, which is *very* expensive and it can be hours or days before a plumber is available.

Gene created an effective alternative to the other options for unclog-ging drains available in the market. The Zip-It Clean is a long, flexible plastic gadget with barbs on it that when placed down the drain and rotated back and forth, grabs the hair and other gunk and removes it when it is pulled out of the drain.

Evaluate the Marketability of Your Idea

When you're working on an idea—as you create, flesh out, and refine the design—it is easy to get caught up in the creativity and the "me" of it. I mean, it is your idea, after all, a product of your intellect and imagination, *your* intellectual property. But if you want your idea to see the light of day, if you want to see it selling in the marketplace, you need to evaluate the marketability of your idea throughout the design process. Because at the end of the day, you'll need to be able to answer yes to the question, "Will it sell?"

That door-opening question is easier to answer than you might think. It's just a matter of finding and evaluating the answers to these questions:

- Does your idea sizzle?
- Who is going to buy your product?
- Why are they going to buy it?
- Where are they going to buy it?
- How much will they be willing to pay for it?

You should already have much of this information, if you've been doing your homework as you work to find and refine your idea. You've found out how your idea stacks up against comparable products as well as where comparable products are sold, how they're packaged and displayed, who buys them, and how much they're selling for. You know which features and benefits your idea offers that comparable products do not. You've assessed the low and high ends of your product category and everything in between, and you know where your idea fits into that market. You know all this from studying the market, talking with industry experts, consulting with your mentor, and researching the Internet and other places, such as trade magazines, trade shows, and trade associations.

But before you take the next big steps of prototyping, patenting, and presenting your idea to potential licensees, it's always a good idea to step back and evaluate, or reevaluate, the marketability of your idea.

For one thing, during the process of finding and fine-tuning your idea, you'll probably discover flaws or opportunities for improvement in your idea. For another, markets change quickly and are affected by external factors such as the economy and emerging technologies. What's good today is not necessarily good tomorrow. So unless you come up with a slam dunk—an idea you can develop and license quickly and easily, like my Michael Jordan Wall Ball—you'll probably need to do more homework and reevaluate the marketability of your idea as you go.

In a perfect world, you would test-market your idea: do a small production run, give it to a group of consumers, collect test data, evaluate it, and tweak your design accordingly. Then you would use this data to help convince a potential licensee to produce your idea and distribute nationwide or worldwide. Test-marketing reduces the risk and is about as good a proof as you can get that an idea will sell. But test-marketing is expensive and time-consuming, and it is simply not practical for most independent product developers.

Just asking the opinions of people you know doesn't work either. The only opinion that really matters is your potential licensee's.

There is one quick and simple way to test an idea or to at least get feedback. I once was able to put a small display of items in a local store. The display included a short survey asking customers what they thought of the products, whether they would buy these products, and which of the designs they liked best. From the returned surveys I was able to determine whether the idea would sell and which designs were the favorites. Of course, not all stores will allow you to do this. It was possible in this case because it was a small retailer in my neighborhood and I knew the store owner. I also gave the store a cash incentive for every completed survey they returned to me.

Another way to test the market is to do a small production run and sell the product on a commerce site such as eBay or Craigslist or with a Google ad linked to your own website. This will give you an idea of whether and how well the idea will sell.

No one has a crystal ball that can tell them with absolute certainty that an idea will sell. Not even Apple Computer, Coca-Cola, General

Motors, and other big corporations that spend millions of dollars on market research and test marketing truly know if something will sell. Besides, people are very fickle. Their tastes change very quickly. So the best you can do is take a close look at what's working and not working in the marketplace, and adjust your course accordingly so you develop an idea that has a good chance of selling.

Most of the time, you can gather all the information you need to answer the question "Will it sell?" using the same methods you used to find your marketable idea and prove its marketability, as discussed in Chapters 4 through 7. It's also a good idea to learn more about the potential buyers of your product. Trade associations and market research firms are good sources of information on consumer buying habits. You can also do an Internet search for information on consumer spending in a specific product category, industry, or demographic (e.g., "teens"). The more you know about the market, the better able you'll be to design a product with the features, benefits, and price point that will sell there. Later, you can also use this information to help convince potential licensees to say yes to your idea.

Just make sure to evaluate your idea objectively using real-world information—based on what you know to be true, not on what you assume or wish to be true. Some product developers have a hard time with this. They get attached to an idea and refuse to adapt it for the market, no matter how clear and compelling the need to do so might be. Or worse, they move forward even when it becomes apparent there is no viable market for their idea. Don't waste your time, money, and talent on go-nowhere ideas. Innovate for the market. Evaluate your idea to verify, qualify, and quantify your potential slice of the pie. Be analytical, not emotional. If your evaluation reveals that your idea will not sell or will not sell well enough to make it worthwhile to a licensee, either let it go or find a way to make it marketable.

Remember, many of the most marketable ideas are small but brilliant twists on existing products, and those simple ideas are often the easiest and fastest to bring to market . . . where they will sell!

Is It Doable?

WHEN A company is even remotely interested in an idea, the two most important questions they'll ask are: "How do we do this?" and "How much is it going to cost?" At the end of the day, no matter how great an idea is, if it can't be manufactured or if it's too difficult or expensive to manufacture, it's not going to get made—at least not by a licensee.

I learned this firsthand when I worked at Worlds of Wonder. We had a team of people from different areas of the company—engineering, marketing, sales—who evaluated ideas from the outside. We had fantastic ideas come in all the time. But no matter how much we loved an idea, if it was going to cost too much to make or if we couldn't do it with our existing production and distribution capabilities, the idea got kicked to the curb.

Since then, I've looked at a lot of patents and accompanying prototypes and technical drawings, and I'm convinced that one of the main reasons so many patents fail to ever see the light of day is because the inventor never even asked these two pivotal questions, much less considered them during the design process. I've seen some really whacky ideas that were clearly conjured up without any idea as to how it would be manufactured and at what cost. If the product cannot be made without a company spending hundreds of thousands of dollars on equipment upgrades, expensive materials, and new technologies, it is highly unlikely any company will be interested in manufacturing it—if it can be done at all.

Companies are only interested in licensing ideas they can:

- Put on their existing production lines quickly and easily, with little or no modification to their manufacturing processes
- Distribute through existing channels in which they already operate or that are closely related to the channels in which they operate
- Produce at a cost and sell at a price that is profitable

It makes absolutely no sense to find this out *after* you've designed the product, prototyped it, filed a provisional patent application, and presented your idea to potential licensees! Your time and resources are valuable, too. You'll save yourself a lot of time, trouble, and heartache and you'll be much more successful in licensing your ideas if you answer these two deal-making, or deal-breaking, questions, "How will it be manufactured?" and "How much will it cost?" *during* your design process.

Is It Doable and Affordable?

To prove to a potential licensee that your idea is doable, you must know how your product will be manufactured and how much it will cost. You don't need to become a manufacturing expert. You just need a basic understanding of the materials, processes, and associated costs involved in manufacturing and packaging your product. That information is easy enough to find.

First of all, if you've done your homework and "shopped" the market to find and design your idea, you've found comparable products and made note of the different materials and technologies used to manufacture them. As discussed, doing this is what tells you that your idea is probably doable and affordable in the first place. Now you just need to prove that.

If the technologies and facilities needed to make your product exist *today*, not only is it easy to find out how to manufacture your idea, it's also easier to license your idea to a manufacturer. A potential licensee will want to do the least amount of extra work and have the least amount of added expenditures to bring your idea to market. If they have to purchase new equipment, modify production processes, source and test new material, train production personnel, engineer new parts, or adapt their manufacturing, packaging, and distribution systems in any other way, it makes it more difficult and expensive for them to do.

The bottom line is, the more able a licensee is to use their existing operations to bring your idea to market, the more likely they are to say yes to your idea. That does not mean your idea needs to be manufactured with *exactly* the same processes and materials as products already on the market. In fact, you absolutely do not want to design a "me-too" product. You—and potential licensees—want your idea to be unique and to add value in ways existing products do not. As you know by now, that usually can be achieved more quickly and easily by making a simple improvement or enhancement to a proven product, by mixing and matching ideas from two different products, or by adding a new technology to a sleeping dinosaur.

That said, some big ideas do get licensed. If an idea has huge market potential but will be somewhat complicated and expensive to manufacture, a potential licensee may well decide it's worth the added trouble and cost. But it will be up to you to provide them with enough information to grasp the market potential of your idea and to gauge their ability and willingness to bring it to market.

Whether your idea is simple or complex, it is imperative to find out whether and how it will be manufactured and at what cost. Otherwise, you'll be hard-pressed to find a licensee willing to even consider it. Beyond that, you'd be foolish to invest *your* time and resources into developing, prototyping, and patenting an idea without first determining whether it is doable and affordable for potential licensees.

How to Determine Manufacturing Methods and Costs

When I was on the evaluation team at Worlds of Wonder, I saw a lot of ideas. Many of them had a wow factor, but only a handful got licensed. One of the main reasons so many great ideas failed to make it to market was because they were too expensive to manufacture. The engineers would give their estimate of the cost to produce it, and no matter how much everyone loved the idea, if it didn't hit a particular price point, it didn't get made.

So it is vitally important for you to find out how your idea can be manufactured and how much it will cost. When a company is interested in your idea, this is the first thing they want to know.

If your idea is simple, it should be easy to find out how to manufacture it and how much it will cost. If your idea is highly technical or calls for materials or production methods that are new or unusual for your product category, you'll probably need to do more extensive research to determine how to manufacture it and how much it will cost. You'll also need to provide more hard evidence to prove to a potential licensee that it's doable and affordable. That's why I recommend pursuing simple ideas at first and waiting until you've got a few licenses under your belt before tackling an idea that's complicated or expensive to manufacture. Either way, get some information and help to determine the method and cost of manufacturing your idea.

The first place to turn for information on how to manufacture your idea and what it will cost is someone who has successfully licensed an idea in this product category or who has firsthand knowledge of manufacturing a similar product. This might be your mentor or another expert you've met through a trade show, trade organization, or trade magazine.

Another way to find out if your idea is doable and affordable is to talk with a *contract manufacturer* that produces similar products. Contract manufacturers exist in every industry, and many of them manufacture products not only for big corporations (maybe potential licensees for your idea) but also for smaller companies and entrepreneurs. Some also manufacture and distribute their own products.

You can find contract manufacturers through a trade association. Trade associations exist to provide information and put people in contact with one another. I recommend contacting a trade association in your industry or product category and asking them for the names and contact information of three or four vendors in your area of interest. For example, if you wanted to talk to manufacturers of guitar picks, you might contact the National Association of Music Merchants (NAMM) for referrals. If you wanted to find manufacturers to talk with about affixing a fold-label to medication packaging, you might contact the Packaging Machinery Manufacturers Institute (PMMI). If you wanted to learn who manufactures bottle caps and sells that equipment, they could tell you. From the association's perspective, giving out a list of vendors may help generate business for their members. Everyone wins.

Once you've got a lead, call the manufacturer and ask for someone in sales. I would say something like, "I'm Stephen Key with Stephen Key Design. I'm working on a special project for a client, and I'd like to send over some drawings and get a price quote."

The sales rep is going to fall all over him- or herself trying to help you and supply you with what you need. Just make sure to send over a *nondisclosure agreement* (NDA), and make sure you've already filed a provisional patent application on your idea. You'll learn more about drawings, prototypes, NDAs, and patents in Chapters 10 to 12.

I usually send over a drawing, and I make sure to include "Patent Pending" on the drawing so they know some intellectual property protection has been filed. It's a little trick I use. I always specify a few different quantities, so I can get a per-unit manufacturing price as well as any volume discounts. For example, I might ask for a price quote on 10,000, 100,000, and 1,000,000 units. The sales rep will go to work for you and come back with a price quote and all this other information to help you because the sales rep wants to get an order! It's brilliant.

Occasionally, I will call contract manufacturers and ask to speak to engineers. If I ask a few basic manufacturing questions and don't ask them to divulge any trade secrets, they're usually very helpful. Sometimes, you can't get them to shut up, because they're so happy to have someone interested in what they're doing.

If the sales rep or the engineer tells you that the company can't manufacture your idea, ask him or her why. This way you can understand the manufacturing process, then redesign if necessary. Then you can either reengineer or redesign the idea. You can also ask if the rep or engineer knows of a company that could produce your idea. Then contact that company to find out how it can be manufactured and at what cost.

Another great resource for finding out how something is manufactured are television programs like the Science Channel's "How It's Made," websites such as http://www.howstuffworks.com, and the free online encyclopedia HSIM (http://howstuffismade.org).

Far too many inventors and independent product developers overlook this step. They design with no knowledge of, and with no regard to, manufacturing. I think that's one of the major reasons most patents aren't worth anything, because the idea cannot be made. Even some industrial design firms are guilty of this, and so they overdesign—developing a product that is too expensive to manufacture. I know this for a fact, because part of my job at Worlds of Wonder was to take those ideas from inventors and industrial designers and then pull my hair out redesigning them for the manufacturing line.

Don't make that mistake! Don't get caught off-guard when a potential licensee asks, "How can we make this?" and "How much will it cost me?" Find out before you present your idea to them. Find out before you take your idea through the whole design process. It will show potential licensees that you are a professional, that you think things through and know how to develop an idea that benefits them. That will go a long way toward getting a company to say yes.

Design for Production and Profit

Only after researching the methods and costs of manufacturing your idea can you determine with any certainty whether your idea is doable. Sometimes, this research will blow your idea right out of the water, making it crystal clear that there is no viable and affordable way to bring your idea to market. Many times, however, you can go back to the drawing board—research and rethink and rework your idea—and come up with ways to make it possible and profitable for companies to manufacture it.

I've had several ideas that did not get licensed, because they were too difficult or expensive to manufacture, and it's always disappointing. But I was able to make that determination by talking with a few contract manufacturers before I had invested a lot of time and money on the idea. On the other hand, I've also been able to rework a number of ideas to lower the cost of producing them. For example, I reworked my spin label to reduce the manufacturing cost by more than 50 percent. Now I am finding renewed licensing opportunities with this product.

A student of ours at inventRight wanted to do something special with toilet paper. Unfortunately, she did all her design work and filed a patent before taking our course and before calling a contract manufacturer to see whether her idea could be made. It couldn't, but they told her what they were capable of. That information enabled her to rethink and rework her idea, file some provisional patents to protect it, and go back to the same company with her redesigned-for-manufacturing idea. Of course, her original patent had no value.

There will be times when you'll have to just give up on an idea. But don't give up easily. In this game, passion and persistence often pay off. So have faith in your ideas but be flexible. Do your homework and be analytical. Design for marketability, manufacturability, and profitability . . . but also follow your heart and trust your gut. If you do that and focus on simple ideas, at least in the beginning, you will be successful in bringing your ideas to market.

10

To Prototype or Not to Prototype

IF YOU'RE following the traditional path of inventing or designing a new product, this is how it goes:

You're working on an idea you're excited about and anxious to get to market. You don't have all the answers yet and you haven't run it by any potential licensees yet, but you're afraid someone is going to steal your idea, so you file for a patent. Just like that, you're $10,000 in the hole, and you don't even know whether your product can be made. Then you build a prototype, or have one engineered and built, only to discover that you didn't do everything right; your product can't be made or doesn't work the way you had envisioned. Now you're a couple thousand dollars more in the hole, but you still have nothing to show potential licensees. So you iron out the kinks, build and test another prototype, and file for another patent. Now you're $20,000 or more in the hole for this idea, and you don't even know if anyone wants to license the thing, much less whether and how you might change it so they *would* want it. Painful to think about, isn't it?

I cannot tell you how many people have $20,000 patent plaques hanging on their walls but no products in the market. And I guarantee their wives and husbands are giving those plaques the evil eye, thinking, *How could you have spent so much money on a stupid idea?* Not only have I seen this painful scenario play out with countless others, I've also lived it. That's why, early in my career, I said, "Forget the prototype, forget the patent!" and found other ways to prove and protect my ideas, so I could avoid needless prototypes and patents.

Shortly after I left Worlds of Wonder, I formed a partnership with Russell Hicks, who had done the illustrations for Teddy Ruxpin. I would come up with an idea, and Russell would draw it out. I'd write up a benefit statement, and we'd create a sell sheet. Sometimes, we'd make an inexpensive mock-up of the idea, photograph it, and incorporate the photo into the sell sheet. Then we would call companies, and if we got a nibble, we would fax them our idea. If they said yes, we'd move forward with the design. If all we got were nos, we'd either go back to the drawing board or let it go, based on what we learned from our research and analysis, which, by the way, included feedback from companies that had rejected us. We didn't worry about fancy prototypes, and we definitely didn't worry about patents.

I've done pretty much the same thing since. In all the ideas I've come up with and pitched to companies, I have never spent more than $100 to make a prototype, and I've licensed ideas without any prototype whatsoever. In large part, I've been able to do this because I like simple ideas that I can easily demonstrate to companies without a complicated and pricey prototype.

Even if your idea is complex, I think it's really important not to spend too much time and money on it until and unless a potential licensee says yes to your idea. To my mind, that is the most important thing: to develop a product that someone wants to bring to market without spending a lot of your own money. So rather than building an expensive prototype that looks like and works like a finished product, I suggest you do what I do: find another effective but inexpensive way to show the benefits of your idea. What I usually do is create a simple and inexpensive model, what I call a "fake" prototype, of my idea. After filing a provisional patent to protect my idea, I trot my fake prototype out to potential licensees to gauge their interest in my idea. I don't even send them the prototype itself; instead, I photograph and include it on my sell sheet or I make a video of someone using it. I figure that if I can show a company how they can make money on my idea, they will pay me to license it—and if they want or need a fancy prototype, sometimes they'll pay for that, too.

Another important thing to remember is that when I submit my simple, inexpensive prototypes to companies, I'm not only fishing for licensing deals, I'm also looking for feedback. I want companies to tell me what they like and dislike about my idea, what works and doesn't work for them, how I can make it more doable, marketable, and profitable for them and ultimately, for me. That way, I can tweak and perfect my design before going the whole nine yards with the design, prototype, and patent.

There is nothing wrong with a nice prototype. I *love* building prototypes. I love seeing, touching, and playing with them. But sometimes you don't need one, at least not a full-on prototype. Sometimes a drawing or a faux prototype is enough to get a company interested in your idea. Certainly, for more complicated ideas, especially if they employ materials or technologies that are new or outside the norm for your product, you'll need a prototype to prove the concept, to prove that it works, or both. Even then, you may not need an expensive engineered and manufactured prototype that is an *exact* clone of your idea. And sometimes, with a simple idea, a killer benefit statement and a kick-ass sell sheet are all you need to seal a deal.

We'll talk about sell sheets, benefit statements, and patents later in the book. For now, let's focus on prototypes.

Types of Prototypes

You almost always need to show potential licensees some kind of physical or visual representation of your idea. You'll probably also need to create a prototype for your own use, as well. When the time is right, one benefit of making a prototype is that it often helps you to discover ways to improve your idea and refine your design. So it's really not a question of whether to prototype or not to prototype. It's a question of *how* to prototype.

There are three types of prototypes:

- "Works-like" prototype
- "Looks-like" prototype
- "Works-like/looks-like" prototype

Works-Like Prototype

A works-like prototype demonstrates how your idea works—mechanically, electronically, chemically, or whatever other working part, process, or technology applies. It is essentially a "proof of concept." It doesn't need to look anything like the finished unit; it can be extremely crude-looking, even ugly. It may not even need to include all the "working" elements of your design; the prototype may only need to demonstrate whatever "working" element of your design is a new technology, unusual for this type of product, or otherwise in question.

The best way to show a works-like prototype to a company is to videotape someone using it, because you don't want to send an ugly prototype to a potential licensee. You just want to prove the concept. And you don't have to make a high-dollar production of it. Just use your home camcorder or iPhone to make the video and then put it up on YouTube, using the feature that enables you to restrict who can view the video.

One of my students, Tom Christensen, made a simple video to demonstrate his idea, the Disclub: a flying disc that a regular person can throw the length of two football fields. Tom made a crude prototype and filmed two people playing with it. In the video, you can't see how rough the prototype is; all you see is that the Disclub does what Tom claimed it could do. Had he sent only his sell sheet and his works-like prototype to potential licensees, it would not have shown the sizzle of his idea. It wouldn't have shown the magic of hurling a disc more than 700 feet! When the sales department at the company saw the video, they told the president they had to have the Disclub. Tom's video proved his concept and got his idea licensed.

Looks-Like Prototype

A looks-like prototype may be either a visual image or a physical representation of your idea. Its purpose, regardless of whichever method you choose, is to provide you with the most effective, and cost-effective, way to show potential licensees what your product will look like. *Visual* means you can see but not touch the object. The visual image may be one-dimensional (i.e., flat; e.g., paper, photograph, digital image) or three-dimensional (e.g., a computer model). *Physical* means a three-dimensional object made out of paper, clay, wood, metal, or another material—something you can actually hold in your hand and evaluate. But a physical prototype doesn't always need to show all sides of your product; for example, the front of the object can look like the real deal, while the backside can be totally flat and blank. You don't always have to show potential licensees the physical model itself. Often, you can simply take a photograph of it.

For many ideas, a looks-like prototype need not be a refined representation of a finished product. Sometimes, a simple drawing or a makeshift mock-up will suffice. A looks-like prototype is really just a sexy drawing or 3-D rendering of what the idea could look like on the store shelf. One of my students created a computer-generated 3-D image of her idea that looked so real that one of the companies she showed it to wanted to order her product right then!

There are times when a refined looks-like prototype of your idea will go a long way with potential licensees. Just make sure that a refined prototype is really to your advantage and that you can afford the time and money to create it. The window of opportunity for new ideas can close very quickly, and you should always look for the least expensive way to effectively "show" your idea.

Works-Like/Looks-Like Prototype

A works-like/looks-like prototype is a functional physical model of what the finished product will both work like and look like. Depending on the complexity of the idea, it can range from a rough model demonstrating some or all of the design elements, to a close model of most or all of the design elements, to an exact model incorporating all of the design elements.

Many independent product developers assume they need to create a prototype that is a very close or exact model of what their idea will work like and look like. That is typically the most complicated and expensive type of prototype to create, and it is usually unnecessary and may even be unwise. Your idea is likely to change several times during your initial design process as well as during the product development process once you've secured a licensee. So before you go this route, make sure you really need a works-like/looks-like prototype to work out the design and to license it to a company. (Remember, you're selling benefits more so than features.)

If you do need to demonstrate both how your idea will work and how it will look, try to find the easiest, most inexpensive way to accomplish that. If possible, model only those elements that really need to be demonstrated. Sometimes, rather than building a works-like/looks-like prototype, it is as effective and easier, faster, and less expensive to create a crude-looking works-like prototype *and* an inexpensive looks-like prototype. That's what I usually do: create a crude prototype that works like it should and a sexy drawing or computer-generated 3-D rendering. Using these two simple prototypes in conjunction gives a one-two punch that proves the idea!

That said, I have licensed ideas without any prototype at all—with only a benefit statement and a sell sheet. I licensed one idea with *only* a benefit statement. It was a product called Sweet Darts, and the benefit statement was, "A plastic dart with a suction cup and the message, 'I'm stuck on you.'"

What is important to remember is that you are always selling benefits and your idea will change. You will make improvements, and potential licensees may request improvements. Before you spend all that money on a prototype, you want to make sure that the benefit of your idea is strong enough.

So my advice is, don't get too caught up in making the perfect prototype. The reality is, most companies don't need or expect you to give them a fancy looks-like/works-like prototype. They understand the cost, processes, resources, and time that go into creating those kinds of prototypes. Do only what you absolutely need to do to show your idea, using the easiest and least expensive way to create an effective prototype of your idea. Then when a company is interested, they can work with you to refine your idea and your prototype. That way, they may pay for all or part of the final product development, prototyping, and testing costs.

Inexpensive Ways to Prototype

There are a number of inexpensive ways to create a looks-like proto-type. Here are some of the most affordable and effective options for creating good-looking prototypes.

"Cannibalized" Mock-Up

This is one of my favorite ways to prototype. You simply find existing items that mimic different elements of your design, take them apart, and glue or fasten them together to create a mock-up of your idea. My prototype of the Michael Jordan Wall Ball is a perfect example of this. I took a poster of Michael Jordan holding a basketball at about his waist-level, glued it to a sheet of cardboard, and cut out the outline of Michael Jordan's image, minus the ball, in roughly the shape of a backboard. I bought an indoor basketball game that Ohio Art already had on the market, removed its backboard, and glued my Michael Jordan backboard to it. This prototype made with cannibalized parts cost about $10 and took about 15 minutes to make. Another way to create a cannibalized prototype is to use clay or spray paint to change the shape, texture, color, or form of an existing product you bought at the store.

Constructed or Sculpted Model

Industrial designers often construct or sculpt models that are shaped like but are not necessarily the same texture or finish as the end product. One of the materials they use to sculpt models is Foamcore. Foamcore is an easy material to scrape away at, and it can be easier to work with than clay. It's fairly expensive, but if your idea is small and can be effectively demonstrated using foam core, it might be a good option for you.

Clay and wood are other materials that can be used to form looks-like models of certain products. Some models are constructed, rather than formed or sculpted, using a variety of materials: wood, metal, rubber, cloth, and so on. This typically requires cutting the materials and then gluing, welding, stapling, nailing, sewing, or otherwise fastening them together.

You don't always have to form or sculpt your prototype from scratch, though. Often, you can change the shape or form of an existing product by adding clay and then spray painting it.

Paper or Cardboard Mock-Up

I use paper and cardboard all the time to make prototypes that illustrate my idea and cost next to nothing to make. You can print or paint paper to look like plastic, wood, metal, glass, stone, and other materials. You can cut and paste it into just about any shape and configuration imaginable: just think of 3-D puzzles and origami, though that might require practice or you might need to hire an artist to do it. It comes in all kinds of colors, and you can change it to any color you want. You can glue photographs, lettering, images, cloth, and other materials to it. You can even create mock packaging for your products with paper or cardboard. I love it! Paper is such a versatile and inexpensive medium for creating prototypes.

Of course, the prototype itself might look kind of funky up close. But here's the trick: just take a photograph of the paper or cardboard prototype. Pictures can be deceiving; they can look like the real deal. Digital photographs can also be altered using graphics software like PhotoShop to make them even more realistic by adding texture or other elements.

A good example of a funky mock-up that did the trick was for my Pocket Pops idea. The concept was a Swiss Army knife with lollipops instead of blades and tools. I made the prototype out of paper and lollipops I bought from the store; then I took a photograph of it. In the photo, the prototype both looked and worked like the real deal.

The Spinformation label was one of my most successful ideas, and I created all the samples for it at the local Kinko's, using color copies, an X-Acto knife, and glue. A year later, it was being demonstrated on TV by Alex Trebek and being sold in Walmart. The employees at Kinko's were amazed to see on TV a product they had watched being built in their store.

Silicone Mold

I've known people to spend tens of thousands of dollars on an injection mold to create a plastic or metal prototype of their idea. Next to paying for a costly patent on an unproven idea, this is the single most costly mistake an independent product developer can make. The manufacturer should pay for the injection mold, not you, and 99 percent of the time, whichever company ends up licensing your idea is going to want to make changes to it before they create the injection mold.

But if you really think you need the perfect prototype and only a mold will do, you don't need to lay out $10,000 to $20,000 for a plastic or metal injection mold. If your idea is small, you often can make a silicone mold on your kitchen table for under $100 worth of materials. Describing how to make a silicone-mold prototype with words alone is akin to teaching a preschooler how to tie his shoes without showing him. You need to watch someone else doing it to really understand how simple it is. At http://www.stephenkey.com/moldmaking, you will find free videos for making silicone molds (and other types of prototypes) as well as resources for purchasing the materials. For now, here's an overview of how to make a silicone-mold prototype:

1. Make a *positive* of your idea. A positive is shaped like and the same size as the finished product would be. You can either sculpt the positive out of clay or carve it out of a block of wood (or hire someone else to do it). An easier way to make a positive is to use an existing product and modify it, if and as needed, so that it is a visual representation of your idea.
2. Build a four-sided box around your positive using Foamcore (poster board) and masking tape, making sure to leave at least one-fourth-inch clearance around all sides of the positive. Leave the top (box lid) open.
3. Pour silicone rubber into the box (with your positive in it). The silicone will fill the empty spaces between your positive and the sides of the box. Let the silicone dry and harden.
4. Turn over the box, and pour silicone into the other side of the mold.

5. After the silicone hardens and dries, remove your positive from the box. The box will now have a hollow cavity in the shape of your positive. This is your mold.

6. Close the mold, and cut a small hole into the top. Use a syringe to inject liquid plastic through the hole and into the hollow cavity of the mold.

7. Wait for the plastic to harden. Open the mold and remove your prototype.

You can usually make several prototypes using the same silicone mold. Sometimes, you can make as many as 50 to 100 prototypes using the same mold. And they look like a professionally made prototype!

Plastic Vacuum Forming

Using a vacuum former to create a thin plastic form of your product is another alternative to injection molding. Many of the clear plastic shells used in packaging—for example, the tray stacked with cookies and placed inside the bag—are made with thermoplastic vacuum forming.

This is how the process works: First, a positive is made out of clay, wood, or some other material. The positive is placed in the vacuum form machine, a flat sheet of thin plastic is laid over the positive, and the machine is turned on. The vacuum former sucks the air downward while it heats up the plastic, causing the plastic to melt over and take the shape of the positive. Once the plastic cools, the positive is removed and the plastic shell is in the shape of your product.

If you are going this route, look for a vacuum or thermoforming company in your area. A small company is your best bet; mom-and-pop and one-person operations tend to be the most accommodating.

3-D Printing/Rapid Prototyping

Many companies and individuals use this method of prototyping, which consists of a part first being designed and dimensioned on a computer. The file is then uploaded to a machine that literally prints a three-dimensional object using liquid plastics that are applied in layers before hardening. There are several rapid-prototyping technologies. Some machines lay down a string of ABS plastic that melts to itself, gradually building up your prototype layer by layer. Another rapid-prototyping technology looks like something out of the movie *Terminator*, with your prototype literally rising up out of a vat of liquid and being hardened at a crosshairs by lasers.

For this type of prototype, you'll need someone to design your prototype on a computer using a computer-aided-design (CAD) program as well as a service provider with a rapid-prototyping machine. If you can't find someone locally, you can mail your CAD file and a return address to a rapid-prototyping service provider, who will return your prototype in the mail.

Rapid prototyping and 3-D printing have been around since the 1980s, but it has become superaffordable only in recent years. Small units often can be printed for less than $100, and this technology can be used to make prototypes in many different materials and colors. Although the 3-D printing/rapid prototyping can be done quite affordably, having someone design the prototype on a computer may not be so easy. With that in mind, make sure this is the best method of prototyping for you. If it is, get several quotes on the CAD and try to find a student or a local professional who's just getting started and may be more willing to give you a good price.

Virtual Model

Virtual models range from a black-and-white pencil drawing on paper, to a full-color digital rendering created using a graphics application such as Adobe Illustrator, to a fully animated, three-dimensional computerized model. Most graphics software and CAD programs are expensive. To use them effectively also requires some artistic skill as well as some training and a lot of practice. So unless you already have those skills and the right software, it is usually wise to find someone who does have that expertise to create your virtual model for you.

If you really need a fancy do-all/show-all prototype and you can afford to spend the time and money to create one or to have one made for you, go for it. But nine times out of ten, you don't need to go to that length. You can usually find an easier, faster, cheaper way to prototype your idea and get it in front of potential licensees via a dynamite sell sheet—especially if you focus on simple ideas with easy-to-demonstrate benefits *and* features.

Whatever kind of prototype you end up with, make sure to incorporate it into your sell sheet. Often, a sell sheet is the only "prototype" a company needs to see to get them interested in licensing your idea.

PART FOUR

Protect Your Idea

You've come up with a great idea and worked hard to perfect it. Now you want to put your stamp of ownership on it to ensure that someone, or some company, doesn't steal your idea out from under you.

But is rushing from the drawing board to the patent office really in your best interests? *Probably not.*

And does a patent really guarantee that you own your idea? *Sometimes not.*

Is there anything else you can do—and anything you should not do—to protect your idea? *Absolutely yes!*

11

The Smart Way to Safeguard Your Idea

Now, IT's important for me to start this conversation about protecting your invention by saying this. If you live outside the United States, you *must* check on the patent, provisional patent, and intellectual property laws in your country.

In the United States *and only in the United States,* patent protection is granted to the "first to invent," meaning the first who conceived of and practiced the invention. In almost all other countries, entitlement to a patent is established by the "first to file," which is awarded based on the date of the application, regardless of the date of the actual invention.

Does this mean that outside the United States you must rush to file a full-fledged patent application? Not necessarily. In many countries (Australia, Japan, the United Kingdom, and China as examples) "provisional" patent applications, which will be discussed in greater detail later in this chapter, allow an inventor to obtain a priority date and a patent pending number, which is valid for one year. A final or complete nonprovisional application must then be filed before the 12-month anniversary of the provisional patent application or the original date will be lost.

Further, in most countries a mutual nondisclosure agreement (NDA) signed by both the inventor and someone with whom the inventor wishes to show or discuss his idea can protect the confidentiality of an invention prior to submitting either a provisional patent application or regular nonprovisional patent application. This is a must in countries where it is first to file.

The bottom line is this. For my international audience, please research the intellectual protection laws in your country! The rest of this chapter is based on my experience in the United States.

The first thing most entrepreneurs and inventors do when they come up with a new product or process or technology is run out and file for a patent. They're so scared someone is going to steal their idea that they want to put their stamp of ownership on it before they show it to a soul. That's understandable. The risk of someone infringing upon your intellectual property rights is real. It happens. Rarely, but it does happen.

What is much more likely to happen, though, is that while you're waiting for a patent to issue, the window of opportunity for your idea will close. Remember: the number one rule of this game is *first to market wins*. So if you don't get your idea to market quickly, someone else probably will. Another entrepreneur or a big company will bring a comparative idea to market and gobble up the lion's share of the pie, leaving you with the crumbs.

Meanwhile, you will have invested $10,000 to $20,000 and waited three or four years for your patent. Anyone who says you can get a patent more quickly or inexpensively than that is out to lunch, because with all the office actions, going back and forth with the patent office, that is what it typically takes: tens of thousands of dollars and a lot of time.

The idea you started with is always different than the idea you end up with. It goes through a lot of changes during its development. So when you file a patent early on, the next thing you know you have to file another patent to cover a design change. As you go along, you make more changes and file more patents. Maybe you find a potential licensee that likes this thing about your idea but not that thing, so you make more changes and file more patents. This old-school method of design-and-patent, design-and-patent, design-and-patent can get very expensive and drag out for years.

There is another, smarter way to protect your intellectual property *while* getting your idea to market. It's called a *provisional patent application* (PPA). Yes, some ideas still need to be patented. But you have more control and flexibility over whether and when to file a patent—as well as who pays for it—than patent attorneys and old-school inventors would have you think.

A Primer on Patenting

Understanding intellectual property rights and how the process works, before you call a patent attorney and before you show your idea to any companies, will save you a lot of time, money, and heartache down the road. My advice is to learn as much as possible about patents, copyrights, and trademarks, especially if you want to make a career out of creating and licensing ideas.

I am not a legal expert, and even if I were, it would take an entire book to cover everything you need to know about patents. So in this chapter I'm going to go over the basics and share some of my and my students' experiences. But I encourage you to seek out other sources of information on patents as well. The U.S. Patent and Trademark Office (http://www.uspto.gov) is an excellent place to start, as are patent offices in other countries. I also recommend David Pressman's books *Patent It Yourself* and *Patent Pending in 24 Hours*.

What Is a Patent?

A patent is a legal property right granted to the person or entity that designs, invents, or cultivates a new (novel) and original (nonobvious) product, process, technology, or service of monetary value. A patent grants the patent holder the exclusive right to make, sell, or use the idea for a specified period of time, during which only the patent holder can authorize (*license*) the manufacture, sale, or use of the idea by another party (*licensee*) or sell outright (*assign*) the idea to another person or entity.

Patents are issued by a federal governing body and are enforceable only in that country. In the United States, patents are issued by the U.S. Patent and Trademark Office (USPTO). Check with your local government agency for details in your specific country.

What Is Patentable?

The USPTO grants three types of patents:

1. Design patents
2. Plant patents
3. Utility patents

Here are some general guidelines on what can be patented:

- A new and original species of plant (*plant patent*) that can be reproduced sexually (with seeds) or asexually (without seeds).
- A reproducible change in the decorative appearance, configuration, ornamental design, or shape of a utilitarian item (*design patent*). For example, a change in the appearance (not the functionality) of a bottle, chair, eyeglass frame, necklace, computer icon, type font.
- A new method of doing business or a new manufacturing process (*utility patent*).
- A useful apparatus, machine, manufactured item, or composition of matter (*utility patent*). The ideas of most entrepreneurs, independent product developers, and small businesses fall under this category.
- Computer programs and mathematical algorithms used in computer programs (*utility patent*). (You cannot patent an abstract mathematical algorithm, only those used in computer software.)

Some ideas require both a utility patent and a design patent. In fact, some ideas may require two or more utility patents, two or more design patents, or both.

How Long Is a Patent Valid?

Design patents protect property rights for a period of 14 years from the date the patent is *granted*, while a plant patent protects property rights for a period of 20 years from the date the patent is *filed*. A utility patent, the most common type of patent, provides property rights for a period of 20 years from the date the patent application is filed. Unlike design and plant patents, however, a utility patent currently requires the patent holder to pay a maintenance fee of $490 at three and a half years, $1,240 at seven and a half years, and $2,055 at eleven and a half years. These fees actually differ depending on whether you have licensed your patent to a small firm (fewer to 500 employees) or a large firm. Failure to pay a maintenance fee results in the termination of the patent.

How Much Does a Patent Cost?

A utility patent costs about $8,000, including attorney fees, though I have known that figure to vary in both directions. A design patent costs less. But keep in mind that most inventions require more than one patent, and a price tag of $10,000 to $20,000 for a single invention is not at all unusual.

How Long Does It Take for a Patent to Be Issued?

Each patent application is reviewed by a patent examiner; this process takes at least 24 months, sometimes more. Rarely is a patent granted immediately upon this single examination. Typically, the examiner comes back to the patent applicant with questions and with requests for additional information, drawings, documentation, or other clarification. In fact, the patent examination process usually consists of two or more rounds of submitting "replies" and then waiting for a response.

After all of that, which can easily take three years, the examiner may reject some of the claims in the patent or reject the patent application outright. You then have the option of filing a request for reconsideration or an appeal, which prolongs the process even further. So you can see how the patent process can easily take three to four years and still not result in a patent being issued.

What Is a Provisional Patent Application?

A provisional patent application (PPA) is a relatively new device that the USPTO began offering in 1995. It is a straightforward application that uses text and drawings to specify how to make and use an idea. PPAs apply only to ideas that fall under the utility patent category. A provisional patent is in force for a period of 12 months, after which you can either file a regular nonprovisional patent application or let it expire.

The Power of PPAs

To be successful in the ideas business, you must show a lot of ideas to a lot of companies. Sending one idea to one company or a couple ideas to a few companies is not enough. A PPA gives you a fast, easy, and affordable way to protect any idea you come up with so you can get your idea in front of as many potential licensees as possible. The whole purpose of a PPA is to test the waters—to get feedback from potential licensees, to test and refine your design, and to make sure your idea is doable and desirable to potential licensees—before you go to the time, trouble, and expense of getting a regular nonprovisional patent.

There are some real advantages to filing a PPA:

- The filing fee is only $110.
- The application is simple enough that you can do it yourself, without an attorney.
- It does not require the formal documentation that a regular nonprovisional patent application requires. You can submit simple drawings and even photographs of rough mock-ups.
- It provides the same legal protection as a regular patent application.
- It is in force for a period of 12 months—plenty of time to do your design work and to find potential licensees.
- You can include a "Patent Pending" notice on documents, draw-ings, sell sheets, and prototypes you present to potential licensees.
- As long as the patent is pending, no potential competitor can access your patent application to rip off your idea. In fact, the USPTO won't even read your provisional patent application until and unless you either file a regular patent application or someone disputes your rights to the idea.
- You can file more than one PPA as you work out the design, pay-ing the application fee for each PPA. Once the design is finalized, you would then consolidate the PPAs into a single nonprovisional patent application.
- It establishes an official patent filing date for your idea. Should you decide to go for a nonprovisional patent, the filing date of your PPA becomes the filing date of your regular patent, thereby extending the duration of your patent from 20 years to 21 years.

Most attorneys will not recommend a PPA. They want to get you for a full patent application. After all, they stand to make more money by pursuing a full patent application. Most argue that they will spend as much time writing a PPA as they will a regular patent application.

You can write your own PPA, but I recommend using the PatentWizard software (http://www.patentwizard.com) from Neustel Law. We use it in my office to write our PPAs, and it works great.

In my experience, PPAs are the most powerful tool anyone can use to protect and license an idea. It safeguards your intellectual property rights, and it enables you to focus on refining your design and finding a licensee. Once you have a PPA in hand, you can and should start calling potential licensees right away, first to get their feedback and then, after you've incorporated that feedback into your design, to secure a license.

But filing a PPA should *not* be your first step! Wait until your idea is ready to present to potential licensees. Do your homework first: prove your idea will sell and can be manufactured. Then file your PPA and start calling companies immediately. If you file for a PPA before doing your homework, you've started the clock on your one year's worth of protection before you were ready to use it, and if your research provides you with negative feedback that discourages you from continuing, you'll have also wasted your application fee.

Inventor's Logbook: A Must-Have to Prove First to Invent

Before you even think about initiating a PPA—in fact, from the moment you first come up with your idea—you should start an "inventor's logbook" and keep it updated. An accurate and detailed logbook is your first line of defense in protecting your idea.

Under U.S. patent law, intellectual property ownership is based upon "first to invent," not first to file a patent. So it is extremely important that you document your idea from the moment you conceive of it, through each design change, and all the way to its final design, licensing, and manufacture. For this purpose, I strongly recommend that you maintain an inventor's logbook for each idea.

Begin by documenting the date you came up with the idea and a detailed description of the idea, including any sketches or mock-ups of the idea. Record and date every consecutive step you take thereafter, in chronological order. Include any variations in or changes to the idea; detailed notes on any testing and prototypes; additional drawings, computer-aided-design renderings, technical specifications, computations, and so on; notes from conversations with industry experts and potential licensees; meetings with patent attorneys; and so on. Cite as many details as possible. Include the full names of any participants in your project and clearly specify their roles. Make sure to also retain your receipts for purchases of any materials used to make prototypes, samples, and sell sheets.

To be legally viable, the logbook must also have the following:

- The journal must be bound so that any removed pages can be detected (a notebook with prenumbered pages is ideal). Never use a loose-leaf binder.
- No lines or pages can be skipped.
- Each entry must be dated and written in ink (not pencil).
- Each entry must be signed and dated by a third party, signifying they understand the contents of that entry. This person can be anyone other than an immediate family member who can read and understand what you've written in your logbook.

The purpose of a logbook is to prove that you created the idea and made improvements to it at specific times. This chronological record of your idea is vital to proving that the idea is 100 percent yours.

If you have not been documenting your idea thus far, backtrack as far as you can remember with accuracy. Include when you got the idea, when you began working on it, what you have done to date, and any specifics you can recall.

When the ownership of an idea is in dispute, the one with the most detailed and precise records is the most likely to win. A well-documented inventor's logbook and a PPA will give you all the protection you need to get your idea in front of potential licensees.

How Margo Licensed Her Idea Without a Patent

Margo came up with a way to label beverage and food items in the refrigerator. One of the things I love about this is that it is a simple idea: basically, rubber bands in an assortment of colors on which you can write your name, a date, or whatever other way you want to label the contents. Margo filed a PPA before she started presenting it to manufacturers. She also consulted with a licensing attorney, who told her no company would touch her idea if she didn't own any intellectual property (which, I later advised her, is not the case). Further, the licensing attorney told Margo that the company she had in mind—which sold in 80 percent of the ideal market for Margo's product—would never pay her royalties on foreign sales, even if her U.S. patent did eventually issue.

Margo called the company anyway. In fact, she called all the major companies in her market, but after speaking with the dominant player, she knew it was a good fit for her idea. She liked how the company operated and how they handled other products. She also felt encouraged by how receptive they were to open innovation and to accepting her sell sheet.

Well, the company did license Margo's idea. What is more, even though she had PPAs in only the United States, she also received royalties on sales in territories in which she had no patent protection. Further, as part of her licensing contract, the company agreed to continuing paying her royalties even if her patents were never issued!

Margo understood that first to market wins. She protected her idea with a provisional patent application. She studied the market, identified the best licensee for her idea, and went for it. She didn't wait three or four years for a patent to issue, and she didn't go to the extreme expense of filing foreign patents. As Margo learned, the company that licensed her idea didn't expect her to file patents in those territories, and they had every intention of paying her royalties on all sales, because as the CEO said, "It's your idea."

Of course, not all licensees are as flexible and generous as the company that licensed Margo's idea, but many are, because they, too, realize the value of first to market. More and more of our inventRight students are licensing their ideas with only a PPA.

How to Get a Patent

For some product categories and industries, you may not ever need to file a regular nonprovisional patent application. In the toy, novelty and gift, and fashion industries, for example, product life cycles are so short that most companies don't require a patent in order to license your idea.

For big ideas, it is best to have some type of intellectual property protection filed. For really big ideas, you will need to file multiple patents, to build a "wall of protection," as my attorney, John Ferrell, always told me. This "wall of protection" sends up red flags to potential intruders that you will protect your intellectual property rights. After all, patents are perceived ownership, and anything can be argued in a court of law. Building a wall of protection around your intellectual property helps keep you out of court by discouraging people from being dishonest.

When it is prudent for you to file a nonprovisional patent application, you can sometimes negotiate with your licensee to pay all or part of the costs associated with filing the patent(s). If you negotiate for the company to pay patent fees on an idea they have licensed from you, you (with your attorneys) still control all filing and office actions.

Whether an idea is big or small, filing and defending a patent takes a lot of time, money, and expertise. I would not even consider filing a nonprovisional patent application myself, and I strongly advise you to retain the services of a patent attorney if and when you need to file a patent for your idea.

Choose the Right Attorney

Not all patent attorneys are created equal. I have 13 patents and have filed dozens of overseas patents, and I have worked with many attorneys over the 30 years I've been licensing my ideas. In my experience, the best way to find an attorney is to get a referral from someone else.

Ask for a referral from someone who has patented an invention, preferably in your product category. If your idea is highly technical or complicated, I also suggest that you hire a patent attorney with expertise in that industry. I cannot emphasize enough how important this is. Knowing patent law is not enough. The attorney also needs to have a working knowledge of the correct terminology and peculiarities of the product category in question so that he or she will understand the design details and the specifics of each patent claim. Hiring an attorney with expertise in the right industry is far more important than hiring one in your neighborhood. The firm I use is a two-hour drive away, and we use e-mail, fax, phone, and express mail services to communicate. In the almost 14 years we've been working together, I've met with them only half a dozen times. Also, make sure the attorney is registered with the USPTO.

Do Your Homework Before Contacting an Attorney

Before calling a patent or licensing attorney, learn as much as you can about the patent application process and about intellectual property protection. Make sure you also know how your idea will be manufactured, and document those manufacturing processes.

Then do a preliminary "prior art" search of issued patents to identify any patented ideas that are similar to yours. Study the prior art to verify that your idea is novel and to identify the differences between those products and yours. You can do this with Google Patents or the USPTO. You don't need to be an expert, but you do need to get some information on how to do this. It takes practice, but before you know it, you will be a pro. That way you can tell your attorney what the claims in your patent application need to say. I make a list, and I annotate the differences between my ideas and other similar ideas out there. I don't want attorneys to be creative; I need to be the one in control, always.

Make sure your inventor's logbook is up-to-date and complete. Create any additional documentation and drawings you may need to fully describe your idea. I do my own drawings, both to save money and to really hone in on my idea. I would not recommend this to everyone, but if you do have the skills to do your own drawings, it will help you to know your idea very well.

Remember: your attorney is only as good as the information you provide to him or her.

Meet with the Attorney and Get a Quote Before Retaining

Most patent attorneys are willing to meet with you briefly for free or for a small fixed fee. During that initial meeting, ask the attorney to give you a rundown of what he or she will do, and ask what it will cost. Get the price quote in writing. Make sure the quote includes *office actions*, because the attorney will most likely need to go back and forth with the USPTO to get your patent issued, the cost of which can add up quickly. Keep in mind that you will be working with the attorney repeatedly, and you will be charged for every phone call, e-mail, fax, and hour spent on your patent application. So be prepared for the actual cost to exceed the quoted price.

If, after the initial meeting, you feel uncomfortable with the patent attorney, or he seems reluctant to represent you, shop around for another one. It's going to be a long and challenging process; you want to be working with someone you feel confident understands your idea and is on your side.

Be an Active Participant in the Process

Once you've retained a patent attorney, the first thing he or she should do is to hire a third party to do a thorough prior-art search. Your attorney will review the prior art carefully, but you need to as well. You may be able to pick up on important things your attorney may miss.

Strategize with your attorney on how best to protect your idea. If you have a highly marketable or highly technical idea, a single patent will not be enough protection; the claims will not be broad enough. I have 13 patents on my Spinformation label, because I realized I needed to build a wall of intellectual property around my idea to discourage someone from designing around it. A good patent attorney can help you to expand the scope of your patent to a certain degree, but you will need to do the homework. Research and brainstorm other ways your idea could be manufactured, as well as every conceivable way the design could be changed and improved upon: different materials, sizes, shapes, configurations, functionality, and other features. Think of other product categories for which your product may be applicable and how you might modify the product's design for that market. Ultimately, you're the expert on your idea, and you will need to figure out all the ways a competitor may try to get around you and provide that information to your attorney. That way, your attorney can include all those possible design and manufacturing variations in your patent applications.

Fight the Good Fight

The first patent I applied for came back from the examiner's office after about 14 months with every single claim rejected. I was crushed. My attorneys weren't fazed at all. They knew this was part of the process, and they knew how to respond. However, I knew my technology better than anyone, and it was up to me to provide my attorneys with the information they needed to prepare the response to that office action.

Essentially, it was a matter of rewriting the patent to get all the terminology just right and then defending it to the examiner. Language, it all came down to language. After the first office actions, I was granted 6 of the 25 claims I'd asked for. After the final go-around, I ended up with 16 of those 25 claims.

Of course, this takes time and money, and it can be emotionally draining. That's why it's important to hire experienced patent attorneys and to provide them with the information they need to go to battle for you.

HOW I OUTSMARTED A BIG CORPORATION AND PROTECTED MY BIG IDEA

I came up with the idea of a rotating label in the mid-1990s after reading an article in the newspaper about how there was never enough information on product labels. As always, I worked out the design, talked to a few industry experts, built a few crude prototypes

continued

using over-the-counter medications I had purchased at Walmart, created a benefit statement and a sell sheet, and started talking to companies. When a packaging exec at a company that provided labels for many of the major players in the packaged goods industries asked, "Do you have a patent on this?" I knew I was on to something big. So I worked with my attorneys to file a couple of patents on my rotating-label idea, which gave 75 percent more space for information than any other label on the market.

Then a friend of mine gave one of my samples to her father, who ended up giving it to one of his golfing buddies, who happened to be the president and CEO of Procter & Gamble. Next thing I knew, I got a call from P&G saying they wanted me to come out to their headquarters in Cincinnati and present my idea to their tech group. *Wow!* I thought, *I've hit the jackpot!* My wife wasn't so sure. Janice has an extensive background in packaging and product development; she had worked at Clorox, and she had actually been offered a job by P&G, the largest packaged goods company in the world. She was worried they wouldn't play fair. But I convinced her to go with me. I needed someone on my team, and this was her world. Figuring manufacturing issues would come up in the meeting, I also invited a representative from a company called Krones, one of the largest manufacturers of processing and labeling equipment in the world, to be part of my team too. I had already established a relationship with them while I was working on the idea.

So the three of us flew to Cincinnati, and I was so exited! Our P&G contact person took us to lunch in the company cafeteria. Afterward, walking across the campus of P&G with the sun on my face, I felt like I had finally arrived. As we walked, I thanked our contact person for lunch. He said, "Steve, remember, there is no such thing as a free lunch." I'll never forget the "I told you so" look on my wife's face when he said that.

We went to a huge meeting room and sat across a huge table from about 20 P&G employees—from marketing, engineering, product development, and legal. I did my part of the presentation. Janice gave her presentation of all the benefits. The guy from Krones got up and explained how easily the labels could be manufactured.

Then the gentleman who took us to lunch slid a piece of paper with some numbers written on it across the table to me and said, "Mr. Key, we're not going to pay you one penny for this idea." The numbers were patent numbers.

Now, when I first came up with the idea, my attorneys had a prior-art search done by a firm in Washington, D.C., that specializes in patent searches. It was such a Forest Gump idea, so simple, that my attorney was sure someone had thought of it before. So he was surprised, and I was pleased, when the search revealed that there was no prior art for a rotating label.

As it turns out, the legal department at P&G found two 40-year-old patents for rotating labels that the Washington firm missed—not similar to mine, exactly like mine. My attorneys confirmed what P&G said, "You'll never get a patent for this. No one's ever going to pay you a penny for it." By that point I had already spent a lot of money on two patents, more money to fly to P&G, and even more money for patent summaries confirming that, yep, not one, but two other people had already invented this idea. I felt pretty foolish. (My attorneys did as well.)

For the next couple of weeks, I was stunned. I went on vacation with my family. But I kept thinking about the label. Something was wrong. If this was such a great idea, if P&G was interested and their attorneys spent all that time trying to avoid paying me for my idea, why weren't the labels on the store shelves? Why hadn't there been any rotating labels on any products ever? It just didn't make sense to me.

So when I got home, I started examining those two 40-year-old patents. I read them over and over and over again. Then it dawned on me! I realized something that those 20 P&G experts didn't see and that my attorneys, one of the premier patent law firms in Silicon

continued

Valley, didn't see: not one claim in either of those patents said *how* to do it—not one!

After I realized there were no claims on how to manufacture a rotating label, I toured labeling facilities throughout the country, observing and asking questions about how fixed labels were applied to containers. Once I understood how labels that didn't rotate were applied to containers, I figured out how to reengineer the labeling process so that labels that rotated could be applied to containers. I couldn't patent my rotating-label idea, but I sure as heck could patent how to make it. And that's exactly what I did!

Today, I have 13 patents on the manufacturing processes used to apply my rotating labels to containers. More than 400 million Spinformation labels have sold to date.

The message here is this: you need to be in control of the situation. You need to understand every aspect of the design, including how to manufacture it. You need to do your homework and make the necessary adjustments, either to the design, the patent, or both, to get your idea to market. If it can't be done, it can't be done. Let it go. Move on to another idea. But don't stop until you've turned over every leaf. Don't give up without a fight.

Procter & Gamble didn't license my rotating label, but that's OK. Many other companies have, and I'm finding additional applications for my Spinformation technology all the time. At the end of the day, P&G gave me the keys to the kingdom by forcing me to take a closer look at my idea. As a result, I figured out how to manufacture—and so patent—my rotating label. Although it was a stressful experience at the time, I realized they were just doing their job. They weren't trying to steal my idea; they just weren't willing to pay me for an idea that they believed had already been patented.

I've been doing this for almost 30 years, and I've presented thousands of ideas to hundreds of different companies. In my experience, most companies are not out to steal ideas. Most are willing to work with you if they're interested in your idea. It's your job to do your homework so that your design is, indeed, *novel* and so that you know how to build a protective wall around your intellectual property.

Another thing to keep in mind is that most of the ideas in my licensing portfolio are simple. The vast majority were licensed using a benefit statement, a sell sheet, and a PPA. The ideas that were patented were paid for by the licensee; I had my attorney file the patent, and the licensee paid for the patent in lieu of an advance.

I actually like that the USPTO is so slow to issue patents, and I love PPAs, because they give you time to test the waters, to see whether your idea has legs, whether a company is going to want to pay you for your idea. When a company is interested in your idea, nine times out of ten they're not concerned about the patent. A "patent pending" provides the perception of ownership, which is usually enough to satisfy most companies, and it provides a sufficient warning to competitors to back off. Ultimately, what companies really care about is getting great ideas to market fast.

12

Control Every Step of the Process

Afterᴇᴿ ʏᴇᴀʀs in the idea business, during which I've developed hundreds of ideas and licensed more than 20 of them, I've learned a few valuable lessons, some, admittedly, the hard way. Hands down, the most important thing I've learned is that I'm the one who has to be at the control panel, every step of the way—from the moment I conceive of an idea until it's brought to market and beyond. Whether I win or lose at this game depends solely on whether I do the right things in the right way and at the right time. That includes asking the right questions of and saying the right things to the right people—and only those people.

So many entrepreneurs, inventors, and independent product developers seem to want to generate an idea and then turn it over to someone else to do all the work for them. Over and again, I've seen otherwise intelligent "idea people" repeat the same dumb pattern: They come up with an idea that gets their creative juices flowing. They work on the design and build prototypes in virtual solitude and often in a vacuum, without doing market research, without talking to industry experts, and without getting feedback from potential licensees. At most, they run the idea past family and friends, who typically have no expertise in developing, manufacturing, and marketing anything, much less that particular product or process. Once they're happy with their design, they file for a patent.

They wait two, three, or four years for their patent to issue, during which they're paying a patent attorney a small fortune to repeatedly revise the patent claims. Then they rely on inventors' services, idea buyer and seller networks, marketing consultants, public relations firms, invention submission companies, invention contests, and the like to sell their ideas for them. But there are no takers. No one buys their idea. No one brings it to market. Or worse, someone else brings a similar idea to market, which is always a risk when you broadcast an idea all over the Internet and publicize it before securing a licensee.

The primary reason so many ideas die on the vine is because the designers didn't stay at the control panel. They either neglected to do their homework and legwork, or they left it to someone else. They didn't consult with the right people at the right time, or they shared their idea with the wrong people at the wrong time.

To protect your idea and to get it to market quickly—which is essential, given that the number one rule of this game is *first to market wins*—you have to control your own destiny. No one is as passionate about your idea as you are. No one is going to work as hard on your idea as you will. No one knows more about your idea or has as much invested in and riding on it as you do. So why in the world would you turn over control of your idea to someone else?

That's one question I can answer with one word: fear. Fear of the unknown. Fear of failure. Most people simply do not know how to design an idea for the market and then license their idea to a company willing and able to bring it to market. They're so afraid of the unknown and they're so afraid of failing at these things in which they have limited or no expertise—which typically are marketing, manufacturing, licensing, and patenting—that they relinquish control of these critical steps in the process. It doesn't make sense, it doesn't work, and *it doesn't have to be that way.*

You can learn how to design for the market. You can find out whether and how to manufacture or otherwise implement your idea. You can be selective in who you work with and ensure that they're working for, and not against, you. You can protect your ideas and profit from them. You can control the entire process of developing and licensing your ideas. How? By following the simple strategies outlined in this book.

Now let's talk about two important facets of protecting your ideas: one that is a necessity for every idea and one that runs counter to what many experts preach and many entrepreneurs practice.

A Necessary Precaution When Sharing Your Idea

When you come up with an idea you're passionate about, it is only natural to want to know what the people closest to you think about it. And of course, you want them to love it! It is also wise to consult with industry experts and a mentor, if you're fortunate enough to have access to either. Just make sure to show your idea only to people you can trust and to keep design details to yourself, your patent attorney, colleagues you can hold in strict confidence, and potential licensees.

It is also critical to have anyone who looks at your idea sign a nondisclosure agreement (NDA) first. When someone or some company signs your NDA, they're promising to keep your idea and every detail about your idea a secret.

My feeling about NDAs have changed over the years. I used to think that as long as I had protected my idea with a provisional patent application (PPA) or a nonprovisional patent, I didn't need to bother with an NDA. Now, after seeing the benefits of how others use NDAs and in using them myself, I think an NDA is necessary whenever you show your idea to anyone other than your immediate family and most trusted friends. Before showing your idea to a potential licensee or to anyone you consult with during the product development and licensing process (e.g., when researching how to manufacture your idea), you should have them sign an NDA.

Most companies will agree to sign an NDA; in fact, most will provide one for you to sign before reviewing your idea. But some potential licensees will balk or flat out refuse to sign an NDA. A company's reason for not wanting an NDA is usually the same as another company's reason for wanting one: to avoid the risk of being sued in the event they already have a similar product in development or may develop a similar product in the future. This is of particular concern to large companies that develop many different products and that look at hundreds or thousands of outside ideas every year. In that case, it is virtually impossible to ensure that none of those other ideas and products will involve information that you feel is "confidential" to your idea but that, in fact, is known by someone else. That is why it's important to include a provision in the contract that limits the scope of the NDA to information that is known to be confidential.

A good NDA will contain these key provisions:

1. The parties agree not to disclose each other's confidential information to others.
2. The parties agree not to use each other's confidential information without compensating the other party.
3. The parties agree to return all documents, information, and prototypes supplied by the other in the event no agreement is reached with regard to the idea.
4. The parties agree that information that is already known to the receiving party or that is known and used by others is not deemed confidential.

Almost all NDAs that a potential licensee will provide you will include these four provisions. An NDA that you provide should include them, as well. Your attorney can draw up an NDA for you to have people sign before showing them your idea, or your attorney can advise you on what to include in your NDA.

If a person or company refuses to sign an NDA, point out that your NDA includes a provision that limits the scope of the contract (see key provision 4). If anyone other than a potential licensee refuses to sign an NDA, do not show them your idea or discuss it with them. If a potential licensee refuses to sign an NDA or provides an NDA that doesn't give you enough protection, you have two choices: (1) walk away, which could reduce your chances of licensing your idea, or (2) offer to modify the NDA in a way that gives the company the flexibility they need and gives you the protection you need.

When to Toot or Silence Your Horn

There is a common misconception running rampant in this era of open innovation that the best way to get your idea to market is to tell the whole world all about it. It's the Information Age version of, *If you build it, they will come,* and it goes something like this: *If you build it and get word out on the Internet, Twitter, TV, and the radio and in every publication you can, some company or investor will come and buy your idea.* It doesn't work that way. Not only is this an inefficient and ineffective strategy for licensing your idea, it also puts your idea at risk of being ripped off or snubbed out.

For one thing, very few, if any, companies and investors go searching the Internet and "tweeting" for ideas to license or fund. Nor do they routinely (if ever) scout social media or any other media for ideas to bring to market. Nor do they frequent (if they visit at all) inventor and product developer forums in search of the next big idea, which in reality is usually a simple idea with big market potential.

These services and media channels may serve a good purpose, but it is not to bring a licensee to your door, despite innumerable claims to the contrary. Sure, if you've already been issued a patent on your idea and listed it with a few respectable "inventions/ideas for sale" listing services, it might get noticed by a product scout who happens to be looking for something along the lines of your idea. It might even result in a licensing deal. But it's a long shot—a very long shot. And it should never be your first or only shot, because your odds of a hit are extremely poor. Infinitesimal.

It is far more effective to go out there and *find* a licensee for your idea. Doing your homework to identify and qualify potential licensees and calling those companies to get their feedback and gauge their interest in your idea gives you a much better shot at licensing your idea. It is a much easier and faster way to get your idea to market. It is also a lot safer.

Some entrepreneurs and independent product developers think, *If enough people could see my idea, surely someone with money will come forward and invest in it. If I could just get some exposure, surely a company will see it and want to license it or pay me a lot of money to buy the patent outright.* In my experience, that's backward thinking. You should publicize your idea *after* you've licensed your idea, not *before*. Until and unless you do license your product and a company is actually bringing it to market, you should *protect* your idea and *not* show it to everybody and his uncle.

Exposing your idea to the wrong people can have dire consequences. It can enable someone or some company to design around your patent and beat you to market with a similar idea. And if you don't use an NDA and don't have a patent or patent pending on your idea, sharing it with anyone—much less, indiscriminately to everyone—is just plain foolish. Also, in other countries outside the United States you can loose your right to patent your invention.

There is also risk in exposing your idea too soon. A product or process can be touted as "new" for a relatively short period of time, and the media only covers new stuff once or twice. So you don't want to toot your horn until your idea is on the market or at least ready for the market. Otherwise, not only could you blow your only opportunity to publicize your idea, you could also give competitors the opportunity to beat you to market with a similar idea.

When the time is right—*after* you've protected *and* licensed your idea—by all means, go toot your horn. Let the world know your idea is out there in the market. Announce it on your website, on your social media pages, and using whatever media channels are available to you. Most licensees will welcome your promotional efforts. Just make sure to coordinate your promotional efforts with theirs.

For example, I was able to get Accudial, one of my Spinformation licensees, on "The Doctors" TV show, where they talked about the benefits of my rotating label. That helped them sell more product, and it helped me to find other licensees. In fact, I use a video clip of that TV segment on my website, as a testimonial of the benefits of my idea, which helps promote it to other potential licensees.

But remember: one of the great things about licensing your ideas is that you can leave the marketing and publicity to your licensees. They do it for you, so you can collect your royalty checks and move on to your next great idea.

To successfully bring an idea to market, you must control every step of the process—from developing your idea to protecting and licensing it. Throughout the process, you must also control who knows about your idea, what they know about it, how you tell them about it, and when. So protect your idea with a PPA and an NDA before showing it to anybody.

And remember: as nice and helpful as kudos and feedback from your inner circle and industry experts might be, the only opinion that really matters is that of the company licensing your idea. So focus on finding and wowing potential licensees—while controlling the process and protecting your idea—using the tools and techniques provided in this book.

PART FIVE

Prepare to Pitch Your Idea

You've come up with a simple idea with big market potential. You've confirmed it can be manufactured or implemented with existing technologies and processes. You've created a drawing, mock-up, or some other kind of visual representation of your idea. And you've filed a provisional patent application (PPA) to protect it. Now it's time to find a licensee that will bring your idea to market.

But before you start calling companies, there are a few simple things you can do to give yourself a huge advantage in selling your idea.

13

Create Sales Tools That Sell Benefits

T HE BIGGEST myth about licensing is that you need to prototype and patent your idea in order to submit it to a potential licensee. While that might be the case with some big ideas, it is definitely not the case with most ideas. To get a potential licensee to say yes to a simple idea, you don't need an expensive prototype that looks like and works like the finished product. An inexpensive visual representation of your idea will do just fine (see Chapter 10). You don't need to spend $10,000 to $20,000 and wait three to four years for a patent to issue. You can protect your idea immediately by filing a $110 provisional patent application (PPA). You don't need to show and sell every feature and every element of your design. All you need to demonstrate are the *benefits* of your idea.

When a company understands what is uniquely beneficial about your idea, they can quickly assess whether it will be profitable for them to bring to market. That is all they care about: whether they can make money on your idea. They don't care if it's the most mind-blowing innovation since the discovery of electricity. If they can't see the benefits of your idea and how they can profit from it, they will not be interested. It's as simple as that.

The two most powerful tools you can use to show and sell the benefits of your idea are:

- A one-line benefit statement
- A one-page sell sheet

What's beautiful about these two benefit-selling tools is that you can create both yourself—quickly, easily, and inexpensively.

Create a Door-Opening Benefit Statement

I can't count how many times I've stood and listened while an entrepreneur or product developer rambled on for 15 to 30 minutes or longer responding to my simple statement, "Tell me about your idea." No matter how long the person talked and how in-depth the description, most of the time I've walked away not knowing how the product would benefit the end user.

No company is going to spend 15 to 30 minutes listening to an idea pitch or 10 to 20 minutes reading a long e-mail. In fact, if you can't articulate how your idea is going to benefit their customers, and by extension, the company, in two minutes or less, you are unlikely to get even five minutes of their time, much less their interest in your idea. They want to know from the get-go, "What's in it for me?" So it is vitally important for you to know precisely what the benefits of your idea are and to be able to articulate them in a clear and concise way.

Here's what I do and what I teach my students to do:

1. Make a list of the benefits your idea offers that similar products do not. Try to come up with at least three. Describe each benefit in one or two sentences.
2. Rank the value of each benefit on a numeric scale—with the benefit having the highest value being number one.
3. Create a one-line benefit statement for the number one benefit of your idea.

This one-line benefit statement is the most powerful sentence you will ever speak or write. Done right, it stops people dead in their tracks. Take this one-line benefit statement for the iPod: "1,000 songs in your pocket."

Believe it or not, I licensed one idea with only a benefit statement. Granted, the idea was simple and could be easily manufactured, so all it took was that one powerful sentence for the company to grasp the idea and see how it would benefit them.

The purpose of a benefit statement, however, is about getting your foot in the door, not about getting a licensing agreement. It's a great way to get a company to open the door so you can step in and wow them with your idea.

Benefit Statements That Opened Doors

Here are some benefit statements that have helped my students and me to license our ideas:

> *This basketball game adds exciting graphics to the backboard and gives you a better return on your money by better utilizing your Michael Jordan license.*
>
> —STEPHEN KEY, LICENSED TO OHIO ART.

The Michael Jordan Wall Ball was on the market for more than 10 years, and it sold more than one million units the first year.

> *My label innovation adds 75% more space to a label.*
>
> —STEPHEN KEY, LICENSED TO CCL LABEL, THE LARGEST PRESSURE-SENSITIVE LABEL MANUFACTURER IN THE WORLD; TO ACCUDIAL PHARMACEUTICALS (FOR CHILDREN'S LIQUID MEDICATION); TO ABC BEVERAGE (FOR DISNEY'S *HANNAH MONTANA* AND *CARS*); AND TO COCA-COLA MEXICO.

My Spinformation rotating labels have sold more than 400 million units worldwide and are used on such products as Rexall Sundown Herbals, Nescafé coffee, Lawry's spices, and Jim Beam DeKuyper Pucker.

> *Throw a disc two football fields.*
>
> —TOM CHRISTENSEN, LICENSED TO SPORTCRAFT.

The Sportcraft brand has become synonymous with family fun. More than 13 million customers a year choose Sportcraft products—and soon they'll be able to buy Tom's Disclub.

> *Don't let stress control your life. Get Relaxium & escape from anxiety!*
>
> —TIMEA CILIBERTI, LICENSED TO NATURE TRADE DIRECT, AS SEEN ON DIRECT-RESPONSE TV ADS.

The most versatile organization system available.

—DARIO ANTONIONI/ORANGE22, LICENSED TO COCOON.

Now his Grid-It! technology is used on more than 200 products—everything from backpacks to handbags, luggage, MacBook covers, and more.

Your guitar will not come apart when the strings are taken off, and it will sound and sustain like never before!

—DWIGHT DEVERAUX/TONEPROS.

Some of the world's top guitarists and the world's best guitar companies currently use TonePros Patent Issued System II Components.

You can still pile and stay organized. Keep your papers neat and organized with PileSmart desktop organizer tray.

—LINDA POLLOCK, LICENSED TO PENDAFLEX.

These are sold in every major office supply store in America.

Skins doors in less than 10 minutes.

—TIM GERHARDS, LICENSED HIS SKIN ZIPPER TOOL, AN AIR-HAMMER-DRIVEN DOOR-SKINNING TOOL, TO STECK INNOVATIVE AUTOBODY TOOLS AND EQUIPMENT.

Clear a clogged drain in less than 30 seconds without harmful chemicals.

—GENE LUOMA, LICENSED TO COBRA PRODUCTS.

His Zip-It Clean tool for unclogging drains is sold in every major retailer in the United States and Canada, including Walmart, Home Depot, Lowe's, Walgreens, and more.

Tips for Writing a Killer Benefit Statement

Though writing a benefit statement may seem simple, it can be quite challenging. I have to admit that my wife often helps me with mine. According to Janice, I tend to "throw everything in but the kitchen sink," and then she has to whittle it down and sharpen it into a short, concise, power-packed one-liner.

Since I can't lend you Janice, here are some tips for creating door-opening benefit statements for all of your ideas:

- **Identify and focus on the one big benefit of your idea.** In most cases, the biggest benefit will be to the end user (the consumer), but in some cases it will be to the manufacturer. One way to articulate this big benefit is to first state a problem and then state your solution.

- **Keep it short.** It should be no more than one line and no more than 25 words.

- **Be concise.** Don't clutter the benefit statement with unnecessary details. Stick to a brief description of your product and its one big benefit. Think of the taglines in TV commercials and in magazine ads that in one short and powerful line tell you what the product is about and make you want to go buy or see it.

- **Be specific.** State precisely how your idea provides that one big benefit. Don't just say it's the best thing since sliced bread; specify what makes it so great. For example, a generic statement such as, "This game is so fun, kids of all ages will want it!" does not tell the company what kind of game it is, how it's different, and why kids will want it. In fact, a generic statement like that not only fails to articulate the benefit of your idea, it also gives companies reason to suspect that your idea has no real value. "The first interactive video game for preschoolers that entertains, teaches, and tickles little funny bones" tells a potential licensee exactly what type of game it is, how it's unique, and why kids (and parents) will want it.

- **Use easy-to-understand language.** Avoid jargon, cutesy catch phrases, and big words that might confuse or annoy the reader or listener. The objective is to communicate the key benefit of your idea, not to show off your vocabulary or entertain.

- **Try out a few.** Come up with four or five different benefits statements. Then pitch them to your family, friends, or mentor. Have someone read them to you, so you can hear how each sounds. Then pick the one that most clearly, concisely, and compellingly articulates the benefit of your idea.

When I first started calling companies about my rotating label, I simply said, "I can add 75 percent more space to your label." When they asked, "How do you do that?" I responded with, "Can I send you a free sample?"

Your one-line benefit statement is the most important thing you'll say to a potential licensee for the first time. Then if they're interested and want to know more, you can provide more information: for example, by briefly describing the other benefits and sending a sell sheet.

Create a Deal-Generating Sell Sheet

A sell sheet is a one-page promotional piece that shows the benefits of your idea in a flash, sort of like a mini-billboard. Just as you can see a billboard while you're driving along the freeway at 60 miles per hour and know exactly what it's selling, so can a sell sheet tell potential licensees exactly what you're selling in 60 seconds flat. Not only that, but a sell sheet will be familiar to the people inside the companies you will approach to license your idea. Companies use sell sheets to introduce new items to wholesale and retail markets, their customers, all the time. If you have a great benefit statement and an effective sell sheet, you don't need to be a sales pro. Your sell sheet will do most of the talking for you!

A sell sheet combines words and images to tell potential licensees exactly what your idea is about and why their customers want it. It is much less expensive and time-consuming to create than a prototype, and it is the most effective sales tool you can use to submit your idea to companies.

That's why I always create a sell sheet *before* I start calling potential licensees. That way, I can call the company and pitch my one-line benefit statement, and if I get a bite, I can offer to fax, e-mail, or mail the sell sheet to them immediately.

The goal of a sell sheet is not to show a potential licensee everything about your idea. It is to sell them on the benefits of your idea so they'll call you back. When you first approach a company, you want to give them only enough information to pique their interest—and you want to make sure *not* to give them any reason to say no. Usually, when a company is interested in an idea, they like most things about it but dislike or are confused about something. If that happens right off the bat, if your sell sheet or benefit statement includes a design detail about your idea that's problematic for the company, they might say no to you without giving it a closer look. But if they get hooked on the major benefit of your idea and discover that one negative later in the game, after they've gotten to know you and your idea better, they are usually more willing to work with you to resolve the issue.

The Makings of a Kick-Ass Sell Sheet

I limit my sell sheets to one page, just a regular sheet of paper. I also limit the amount of information and images on the page. Potential licensees need to understand your idea and the benefits of your idea quickly. If your sell sheet is longer than one page, it will usually get tossed in the trash. If it's too cluttered, it may not articulate the major benefits of your idea clearly or quickly enough.

Every sell sheet should include these critical components:

- Your one-line benefit statement
- A visual representation of your idea
- Your contact information: your name or business name as well as your e-mail address and business phone number
- A few additional benefits of your idea—as concise and compelling as your big benefit statement
- Evidence of your intellectual property protection, in small type in the lower corner: "Patent Pending" or the patent number, if issued; never list an application number

The most important component of your sell sheet is your one-line benefit statement that succinctly articulates the big benefit of your idea. This powerful one-liner should be in large and bold type. It should be prominently displayed, usually at the top or along the bottom of the page, so that your eyes are immediately drawn to that statement.

The visual representation of your idea should be the other prominent element on your sell sheet. There are many different ways to "show" the benefits of an idea on a sell sheet, and you'll need to decide which type of image works best for you and your idea. For some ideas, a single line drawing, illustration, computer-generated 3-D image, or a photograph of a mock-up of your idea is all you need. For some ideas, a photograph of someone using your product may be the most effective way to demonstrate your idea's benefit. For other ideas, you may need to create a storyboard: a series of two or more images that tell a story in pictures, sort of like a cartoon strip. Whatever type of image you decide to use, just make sure that it depicts the big benefit of your idea.

Remember, you don't need to spend a lot of money building a looks-like/works-like prototype that is an exact working replica of your finished product. In Chapter 10 we discussed several inexpensive but effective ways to model your idea or to create a visual representation of your idea. Just make sure that the visual of your idea looks good and clearly shows the benefit of your idea.

The best way to create a professional-looking sell sheet is with graphic art software such as Adobe Photoshop, which is expensive, or with less expensive software such as Corel PaintShop Photo Pro. But you can also create a good-looking sell sheet using Microsoft Word or a similar program. Creating a sell sheet on your computer gives you a lot of design flexibility. After you've created a visual representation of your idea, you just import it to your sell sheet, where you can resize it or move it to different parts of the page to see what looks best. For the words, you can use different fonts, sizes, and colors as well as bold and italics.

If your idea is highly technical, you might want or even need to include a technical illustration on your sell sheet. However, in my experience, it is better to keep it simple, and a rendering of the finished product is usually best. The purpose of the sell sheet is to show the benefits of your idea, not to show every feature of your idea and how it works.

Submitting Your Sell Sheet to Potential Licensees

Never send a sell sheet to a company without first getting permission from the company. Otherwise, it will be considered junk mail. Call the company first, pitch your idea using your one-line benefit statement, and then if they seem interested, ask, "Can I send you a one-page description of my idea?" If they say yes, get your sell sheet to them immediately.

When you send your sell sheet, always include a cover letter and a business card. The cover letter should introduce who you are and thank the company for reviewing your product.

For 25 years, I have sent my sell sheets directly to the company using FedEx. I used to send overnight, but when you're mailing sell sheets to 10 potential licensees and sending multiple copies to each company (so everyone involved has a copy; something you can't do with a prototype), that gets expensive. So now I use second-day service. I used to sometimes fax sell sheets and would follow up with FedEx so I could send more than one copy. These days, I often send my sell sheets via e-mail.

Most of my students send their sell sheets to potential licensees electronically, as an e-mail attachment. If you take this route, make sure to use a document format that the company can open, read, and print but cannot change in any way.

The only two types of electronic files I recommend for sell sheets are HTML files and PDF files. Most versions of Microsoft Word and similar programs allow you to "save" a document as an HTML Web page and to password-protect it. Then you can either send the HTML file as an e-mail attachment or upload it to a Web page, which is what I prefer because you can send someone to the site to check out the sell sheet while you're talking with that person on the phone.

PDF files are electronic files that can be opened, viewed, and printed using Adobe Reader—a free program that is usually provided on new computers. It can also be downloaded for free from the Adobe website. You cannot create a PDF file with Adobe Reader. To create a PDF file, you need a PDF writer. Adobe sells PDF writing software (called Acrobat), which is kind of pricey. You can also download free and inexpensive PDF writers from the Internet. One free PDF writer I've used is CutePDF (http://www.cutepdf.com); it is easy to use and the instructions are easy to follow. Also, if you are using Microsoft Word 2007 or later you can save your document as a PDF.

Why spend a small fortune and several years of your life trying to license your idea the conventional way—with a fancy prototype and expensive patent—when there is a faster, cheaper, and simpler way to bring your idea to market? Remember: getting a potential licensee to say yes is all about selling them on the benefits of your idea. And the best sales tools for selling benefits are your one-line benefit statement and your one-page sell sheet. I have licensed more than 20 of my ideas using only a benefit statement, a sell sheet, an inexpensive prototype, and a PPA. Most of my inventRight students have licensed their ideas the same way. You can too.

Get in the Game Without Quitting Your Job

CONTRARY TO popular belief, you can play with the big guys—and be taken seriously—without having to go through the time and cost of starting a full-on business. With my 10-step strategy for creating and licensing ideas, you can do this as a hobby or as a very part-time second job, or you can slowly build it up to a full-time profession that allows plenty of time for your family, friends, and other interests. You can even live the licensing dream on a shoestring by creating a business image and by outsourcing some of your work to young professionals and students.

Fit the Dream into Your Life

I am the quintessential dreamer. The creative type. A kid at heart. In my early twenties, I decided I wanted to make a profession out of creating and licensing my ideas, which I have been fortunate enough and have worked hard enough to do. So I understand, I really understand, how tempting it can be to throw caution to the wind and just go for it. But that would be a bad idea, a very bad idea.

I cannot say this often and strongly enough: do not quit your day job. Do not mortgage your house to the hilt, go into debt, and use up your kids' college education funds and your retirement funds. Do not let creating and licensing your ideas consume your resources—or you. The whole point of the licensing lifestyle is to have the time, resources, energy, and presence of mind to enjoy your life and your family, *not* to diminish or neglect either. It's all about making your life better, and that means creating a healthy balance between work and play, between work and family, and between work and rest.

It has taken me awhile to learn some of these lessons, and I want you to avoid the mistakes I made! There was a time when all I talked about, all I thought about, all I did with my family had something to do with my ideas. I remember seeing a glazed-over look in their eyes. I have changed. I have learned to make my family a priority in every way: in providing for their material needs, in giving them my time and attention, and in listening to and supporting their dreams. In turn, they do the same for me.

Another thing I have done and recommend you do is to connect with other creative people with similar interests. Find a group of entrepreneurs or inventors to meet and talk with regularly. Sharing ideas and enthusiasm with like minds will give you a great outlet, and it will give your family a little break from all that passion. Being passionate about your idea is a good thing, but not if it's your only thing and the only thing your family hears about.

Coincidentally, I recently met another passionate inventor whose wife divorced him because he got so caught up chasing his dream. He also spent $250,000 on prototypes and patents, which may well have been money that either he or his wife couldn't afford to spend or she didn't want him to spend in that way.

The sad thing is, he didn't *have* to do it that way. If he had followed my approach to licensing ideas, he might have licensed his idea by now—at a fraction of the cost and time he's already invested. And he might have saved his marriage.

Janice and I just celebrated our 22nd wedding anniversary. Had I been foolish enough to put our financial security at risk and to put my dream before our life together, she would have left me years ago. I found a better way to do this, and we're all the better for it. I've also helped many other people use those same tools and techniques to live their dreams without turning their lives upside-down.

How Two Drummers Banged Out a Winning Idea in Record Time

Two of my inventRight students have taken it one step further. Jeff and Mark not only have full-time jobs, they are also part-time musicians (drummers). They have been friends for 30 years, but live 80 miles apart in Southern California, where commuting 10 miles can take 60 minutes in rush-hour traffic. They are both married and have children. So they don't have much time to meet face-to-face. But they had an idea for a new take on an old percussion instrument—maracas, or rumba shakers.

Jeff and Mark developed a new take on this sleeping dinosaur, which their benefit statement describes better than I can: "A new shaker innovation that provides multiple sound qualities, precision control, and the ability to create complex rhythmic patterns in one compact instrument." Using the methods they learned at inventRight, these two friends developed their idea over the phone while commuting to and from work (using handless mobile phones, of course), sometimes at lunchtime, and on the weekend. They developed an inexpensive prototype, filed a provisional patent application (PPA), created a sell sheet, and recorded a video that they put on YouTube with password protection.

They called potential licensees the same way they developed the product: on their handless cell phones driving to and from work and at lunchtime. Four months and $800 later, they had a licensing deal with Latin Percussion, the largest percussion instrument manufacturer in the music industry.

Jeff and Mark have a new motto: "Invent yourself out of a day job one idea at a time." They're well on their way. You can be, too, by taking it one idea—and one step—at a time.

Now let's look at a couple ways to bring you closer to living the licensing dream.

Create a Professional Image

When you're pitching ideas to potential licensees, it is imperative that you present yourself and your idea in a professional manner.

Everything you present to a company—from your business card to your benefit statement and sell sheet—must be pitch-perfect. These are the tools that will get you in the door and get a company interested in your idea, and they need to pop!

Companies want to know they're dealing with a legitimate business, with a professional who knows how to develop an idea for the market. A potential licensee is far more likely to take you and your idea seriously if you present yourself as the entrepreneur or owner of a design firm, rather than as a weekend inventor who comes up with kooky ideas for a hobby or as a regular guy or gal who happened to come up with an idea (the implication being, your one and only idea).

That does not mean you have to go out and lease and furnish an office, hire an assistant, and get a fancy brochure made. Nor do you have to hire an attorney and form a corporation. Once your ideas start getting licensed, you can speak with the Small Business Association (SBA) in the United States and Canada, the FSB in the United Kingdom, or an attorney to figure out the best way to structure your business. In the beginning and for the purposes of contacting and pitching your idea to potential licensees, the only thing you need to have is the *appearance* of a legitimate business.

You can cultivate an air of legitimacy with a professional website, business cards, letterhead, a dedicated phone line, and a dedicated business address. Your business phone can be a mobile phone, and your business address can be a post office box. Presenting yourself as a legitimate business conveys to potential licensees that you are a professional who understands the business of developing and licensing ideas. That provides a benefit to them and an advantage to you.

Outsource Without Breaking the Bank

Few entrepreneurs and independent product developers have the skills to do everything themselves. Truth be told, few want to. Most either can't or don't want to come up with and develop marketable ideas *and* design good-looking business cards and letterhead, *and* write good benefit statements and cover letters, *and* build good prototypes, *and* create effective sell sheets, *and* do all the other tasks involved in developing and licensing ideas. And you probably can't, either.

Even if you can and want to do all those things, doing everything yourself may not be the best use of your time and abilities. To succeed at this game, you need to have a lot of lines in the water all the time. You need to be constantly coming up with new ideas and casting them out to potential licensees. Outsourcing the tasks you don't do well or don't enjoy, or that simply take too much of your time, enables you to focus on finding and developing ideas.

Now you could hire a top-notch professional copywriter or an advertising firm to come up with a benefit statement and content for your sell sheet. While you're at it, you could also hire a professional graphic artist to design your sell sheet, business cards, and business stationery; a Web designer for your website; an industrial engineer or model maker for your prototype; and a commercial photographer to take a picture of your prototype. The more experienced the professional, the more you can expect to pay for the services. So if you were to hire everything out to top-notch pros, it could quickly add up to thousands of dollars.

A more cost-effective and time-efficient option is to take my approach: do as much as you *want* to do and *can* do well yourself. Then outsource everything else to college students and independent contractors who are able to provide good service and willing to give you a better price than design firms or more experienced professionals.

I hire students all the time to help me with my sell sheets. For example, I pay $20 to $30 for a drawing that takes an art student an hour or two to draw. They're happy to make a few bucks and to have something for their portfolios. My assistant does all my photography and graphic design work now, but I used to hire college students for those tasks as well.

You can also hire students and independent contractors (e.g., industrial engineers) to create prototypes, specifically if you need a technical drawing, a 3-D rendering created with computer-aided-design (CAD) software, or a clay model. You can even hire someone to pitch your idea to companies, if you really hate "selling" and think a professional salesperson or a product scout might do a better job of licensing your idea than you would.

As I've gotten older, I've realized that I want to focus more on creating and developing ideas and less on doing all the other stuff I need to sell my ideas. So I've built a team of talented people to help me create prototypes and sell sheets, protect my intellectual property, maintain my website, and provide other assistance. I'm selective in whom I work with and am very hands-on. I make sure we're all on the same page and that it's a win-win business partnership.

What's important is that you find the right people to do whatever tasks you need or want to outsource—whether it's creating a logo for your business card, a technical drawing of your idea, or your sell sheet—so that you can bring your ideas to market as quickly, effectively, and economically as possible. In my opinion, the right person for the job is someone who is competent, professional, trustworthy, and affordable.

Where to Find Help

People with skills in CAD, copywriting, graphic design, illustration, industrial design, model making, photography, prototyping, and other services are easy to find.

Here are the types of people to whom you can outsource those tasks you don't want to do or can't do yourself:

- 3-D animator
- 3-D modeling expert
- CAD engineer
- Electrical engineer
- Electrical engineering college student
- Graphic artist
- Graphic arts college or high school student
- Illustrator
- Fine arts (illustration) college or high school student
- Industrial designer
- Industrial design college student
- Industrial technology college student
- Machinist
- Mechanical engineer

- Mechanical engineering college student
- Model maker
- Prototype specialist

For most things, I prefer outsourcing to students and young professionals, because they are usually affordable, eager to do a good job, and have that entrepreneurial spirit. A great way to find talented students is to call a professor and ask if they have any students who are outstanding in whatever field I need help with. The instructor will often refer one or two students to me. Other times, the instructor will announce my request to the whole class or post it on a job board. I usually get great work at a fraction of the price, and the college students appreciate the money, the addition to their portfolio, and the confidence I've placed in them.

But with the Internet, you don't even need to call or go to the local college to get a sell sheet or a technical drawing done. You can go to a freelance website and outsource to freelancers on the other side of the country, or in Canada, India, South America, or anywhere.

Here are a few places to locate skilled talent to do whatever work you need help with:

- Local companies providing the services you need—for example, advertising and marketing agency, industrial engineering firm, commercial photography, and so on
- Local independent contractors—for example, graphic artists, industrial engineers, and illustrators
- Websites where people can post and bid on freelance projects, such as http://www.elance.com and http://www.guru.com
- Community colleges, universities, design schools, and trade schools in your area

How to Outsource Your Work

Before hiring someone, you should always get some evidence that the person has the ability to do the work you need done. Just because someone has a computer and CAD software or a PhotoShop program doesn't mean he or she knows how to use them properly and is a good designer. Ask for a résumé as well as a portfolio or samples of the person's work. Ask for and check references. Although students and young professionals probably won't have a lot of work experience and references, they should have at least a few portfolio pieces and references from their teachers, if not also clients or employers.

Always get price quotes up front, too, and from at least three different sources for every project. Prices can vary dramatically, and a high price is not always (or usually) an indication of quality. You can usually get great work at a reasonable or even low cost, especially if you use my method of outsourcing to students and young professionals.

Before you provide a potential vendor with any details, drawings, or mock-ups of your idea, have them sign a work-for-hire agreement (WFH). It should include language about your being the sole (100 percent) owner of the idea; that way, if the person you've hired makes any change to your idea or product, they are not considered a coinventor. The WFH should also include a confidentiality statement that specifies the person cannot ever reveal anything about your idea to anyone or use your idea in any way without your explicit written permission.

Finally, communicate with your service providers and manage the process closely. Provide them with all the information and direction they need to do the project, be accessible in the event they have questions or concerns, and check in frequently. For more complex projects, you might want to set milestones and check the progress at each one. This enables you to catch and correct problems before things get too far gone or to find another source if you discover you've hired the wrong person for the job.

There are so many options for outsourcing your sell sheets, prototypes, and other projects. I love that you can outsource your work all over the world, as well as to talented students and young professionals who need the money and the experience right in your community. You can outsource your whole team, and if you choose carefully, you can get the professional help you need at an affordable price. That way, you can better manage your time, your costs, and the whole product development and licensing process.

PART SIX

Submit Your Idea to Potential Licensees

You've followed all the right steps to bring your idea to life: created a unique idea and designed it for the market, proved it can be manufactured and will sell, protected your intellectual property, and created a benefit statement, a sell sheet, and a professional business image. Now it's time to pitch your idea to potential licensees.

This is when many product developers choke. Why? Because they don't know where to go, whom to talk with, and what to say. They're intimidated by the mere thought of knocking on the doors of big companies.

But it doesn't have to be that way. There are simple ways to get your idea into the right hands and get you one big step closer to having a company saying yes to your idea.

Kick Fear to the Curb

IF YOU'RE like most people, the biggest obstacle standing between you and getting your idea to market is fear. That is understandable, especially if you're new to the licensing game. The truth is, everyone has fear. In fact, every successful entrepreneur and independent product developer I know, myself included, has had multiple fears. But here's the other truth: fear is surmountable. Because in the vast majority of cases, fear is just "false evidence appearing real."

I've found that the best way to dispel fear is with preparation and persistence. Studying the game, getting ready for the game, and practicing the game not only will give you more confidence, but also will greatly improve your batting average. The more you know and the more experience you get under your belt, the less fear you'll have and the more success you'll have. Remember: this is a numbers game. No one, not even the most brilliant and prolific creative minds on the planet, hits a winner every time or even every tenth time. To be successful and enjoy the full fruits of the licensing lifestyle, you need to generate lots of ideas. So you need to get smart, get rid of the fear, and get many ideas in front of many companies.

Now let's take a look at the most common *fears* preventing people from even trying to rent out their ideas and why you can kick each one of them to the curb.

Fear of Getting Ripped Off

One of the biggest fears people have about licensing is that a big company, or an employee within a company, is going to steal their idea. For some people it is a paralyzing fear, and it is largely unfounded. Every once in a while you'll hear a story about a David claiming that a Goliath has lifted his idea. But usually that's all it is: a *story*, with little or no truth to it. In those rare instances when a company does stake claim to an idea that is similar to someone else's idea, it usually turns out to be a misunderstanding or mistake that is resolved to the mutual satisfaction of both parties. It is not in the best interests of any company to pilfer ideas. Both the odds and costs of getting caught are high. It's not worth it, and it's not necessary.

One reason it's unwise for companies to steal ideas is because today with the Internet, the little guy has a huge voice. If something were to go wrong in your dealings with a licensee or would-be licensee, you could go online and use blogs, forums, and social media networks to post complaints and warnings, telling the whole wide world about it. So trying to steal an idea would be a public relations nightmare for a company.

But if you suspect a company is trying to steal your idea, make sure you have all the facts straight and think it through carefully before you start blowing whistles. Be careful not to make false statements or to say anything that might slander the company or anyone associated with it. You don't want them to file a libel suit against you. You also don't want to cry wolf or make a fuss too many times, because then other companies won't want to work with you.

No company wants to go to court over a patent infringement or other intellectual property dispute. Litigation is expensive and time-consuming. No matter how deep a big company's pockets might be, they don't want to spend time and money trying to prove an idea is theirs and not someone else's. They need their resources for other things such as research and development (R&D), marketing and distribution, salaries and benefits, and all the other things involved in running their business.

Some patent attorneys would like you to think that big companies are in the habit of mowing over the little guys. These attorneys want you to be fearful because they want your business. They want you to be so scared of getting ripped off that you'll pay them to file patents for you. You should never get a patent out of fear. First of all, as discussed earlier, you can protect your idea with a $110 provisional patent application (PPA) for up to 12 months, while you're showing it to manufacturers to get feedback and secure a licensing deal. Second— and I can't state this often or strongly enough—companies are *not* out to steal your ideas. It happens so rarely that you are a hundred times more likely to have your identity stolen (1 in 200) than you are to have one of your ideas stolen.

What happens more often is that two people will be working on the same or a similar idea at the same time. So an independent product developer could approach a manufacturer with an idea that is close to an idea the company's R&D team is already working on. When that happens, it can actually pose a bigger risk to the company than to you. For example, when I submitted my Michael Jordan indoor basketball backboard idea to Ohio Art, I also submitted a few other ideas. Here is an excerpt from the letter I received from my contact at Ohio Art:

> *Dear Stephen:*
> *As per our telephone conversation, I am returning all of the items that you sent to me for review with the exception of the Michael Jordan Poster Basketball game.*
> *I will not be reviewing any of the other items with our Design Staff due to the fact that we have been very actively working in this area in the past, and I fear that they could be influenced by some- thing you presented, and I certainly do not want that to happen. As a matter of fact, we may be marketing some of these items in the future and you must understand that we have been working in this area and would have no obligation in the event that we do market some products of this type. . . .*

Another reason why it would be unwise for companies to steal an idea is because they need open innovation to compete in today's fast-changing global marketplace. Most companies today understand the value of the multiplying effect: of having people outside their walls working for them. It's like having an R&D team of thousands of people without the overhead. If a company were to start taking ideas without paying for them, the news would spread like wildfire and no designers in their right mind would submit ideas to them.

I think the fear of getting ripped off is overblown. I've submitted thousands of ideas over the years, and only once has a company used my idea without licensing it. (I'll tell you more about that in Chapter 19.) Even then, it was more a matter of miscommunication and confusion than deliberate theft. If you've used one of the intellectual-property protection tools provided by the U.S. Patent and Trademark Office (USPTO) or your appropriate government body, and done your homework to find the right companies to approach with your idea, you'll be fine.

Fear of Cold-Calling

Everyone feels at least some apprehension about calling someone they don't know, and for some people, it is downright terrifying. The first thing you can do to help dispel that fear is to realize you're not really cold-calling; you're presenting your idea—an idea that, if you've done your homework, you know has value to the company. If you've nailed your one-line benefit statement and your one-page sell sheet, your idea will sell itself. All you have to do is find the right company and get your foot in the door.

The only successful way I have found to do that is to call the company and actually speak to someone with the authority to review ideas. If you just send an e-mail or letter to someone you don't know—or worse, to "The Vice President of Product Development" or to "R&D," or the worst of all, "To Whom It May Concern"—you will never get the response you want. Almost every day, I hear from a student or client who is afraid to make phone calls. They'll say things like, "I've sent hundreds of e-mails, but no one responds," and "I've been sending letters and drawings, but I haven't heard back from anyone." What a surprise! To a busy executive, an unsolicited submission from a stranger is just more junk mail. How much junk mail do you read?

So if you want to submit your ideas to potential licensees, you are going to have to bite the bullet and call them directly. I know what you're thinking and what you've been told. I've heard every objection to cold-calling in the book: *People who work at big companies are too busy to talk with little guys like me. It's impossible to get past the gatekeepers to the real decision makers. Everybody prefers e-mail these days.* Yada, yada, yada.

Here's the reality: these guys need you! They are looking for ideas. There are project managers everywhere who are so busy putting out fires that when you come along with a great idea that's going to make the company money and make them look like a hero, they're going to love you. If they get a bonus or a promotion because of your idea, they might even start coming to you for ideas.

So before you make those calls, get yourself in the right frame of mind. Believe in yourself and in your idea. Know the benefits the company will derive from your idea. Practice your one-line benefit statement over and over again. Be yourself, and let your passion for your idea shine through. Your confidence and enthusiasm will jump right through the phone, and it will make the person you're talking with want to know more about your idea.

Another thing that may help relieve your anxiety about cold-calling is to remember that the purpose of that first call is not to sell your idea. It's to introduce yourself, to present the big benefit of your idea (e.g., a solution to a problem, how the company can make money), and to ask whether the company would like to know more. So the call should be brief: get on, make your point, and get off. Then follow up with a sell sheet and brief cover letter if the contact says yes to reviewing your idea.

Here's another fear-squelching tip: when you're first starting out in this game, don't call your top choices of potential licensees first. Call the lesser choices and long shots, so you get some practice. My first call is usually a little rough, the second is better, and by the third and fourth, I've found my voice and lost my fear.

Knowing your benefits and practicing your cold-calling spiel will go a long way toward alleviating your fear of cold-calling.

Fear of Fumbling

In that first call to a potential licensee, your goal is to present your idea and sell its benefits. Their goal is to determine very quickly whether your idea is a potential fit for their company. So they're likely to ask questions and need additional information. It is the fear of not knowing all the right answers, of misspeaking or making a mistake, and of coming across like a bumbling idiot that stops many entrepreneurs and independent product developers dead in their tracks.

The first step to overcoming this fear is realizing this: you're never going to have all the answers. No one does, and no one expects you to. If I don't have an answer, I don't lie or pretend I do. Instead, I say, "I have to get back to you on that." Then I reach out to my network for the answers.

Actually, that's the second step. The first step is to do your homework and your legwork before you make these calls, by:

- Studying the marketplace
- Talking to someone who has done it before
- Knowing how your idea stacks up against similar products—in terms of features, benefit, and sales price
- Finding out whether and how your idea will be produced (or implemented, if it is a process or service) and at what cost
- Having a basic understanding of patents, and filing a provisional patent application (PPA) or another type of intellectual-property protection
- Researching each potential licensee to get a good understanding of their products and customers
- Knowing the big benefit and all the other benefits of your idea
- Having your one-line benefit statement and your sell sheet ready to go

Go over all of this information and materials, and practice your cold-call pitch. That way, you will be as informed and prepared as possible for the manufacturer's questions and queries.

Everything in this book will help prepare you for all of your dealings with potential licensees. That preparation will help allay the fear of not being able to answer an important question or to provide important information when asked.

But sooner or later, someone is going to ask something you can't provide on the spot. Don't panic! It's OK not to have all the answers, and it's better to be honest about that and get back to them with the right answer than it is to fake it or give faulty information. If a company representative ever asks for something you're unsure of, always give yourself a day or two to gather the information, your thoughts, and your confidence before getting back to them. When this happens to me (and it still does, after many years of cold-calling), I either call or e-mail the answers back in 24 to 36 hours. That's enough time to pull myself together and come back swinging, but not so much time that they start to lose interest or question my professionalism.

Here's another fear-dispelling tip: keep good records. Maintain a detailed, up-to-date inventor's logbook as explained in Chapter 11. File all your research notes, drawings, receipts, sell sheets, and other materials in the same place. Retain a copy of every e-mail, fax, and letter you send and receive from each potential licensee, and keep a written record of every phone call and meeting you have with each company, making sure to date each entry and briefly note the outcome. A good paper trail will give you the backup you need to both present and protect your idea—killing two fears with one stone: the fear of messing up *and* the fear of getting ripped off. If you do fumble when pitching your idea to a potential licensee, as everyone does once in a while, be able to laugh at yourself and keep going, perhaps making sure to first review your notes more carefully next time. If you ever do find yourself in court—which I hope never happens and it rarely does—all this documentation will come in handy. The one and only time I had to defend my idea in federal court (see Chapter 19), I had to provide evidence of certain events and timelines.

Fear of Rejection

Rejection is always hard to swallow for everyone. But I really think that the fear of being rejected can be worse than actually being rejected—

especially when the fear of being told no inhibits you from giving companies the opportunity to say yes to your idea.

One way to reduce fear is to face it. And let's face it: rejection is inevitable in this game. You're going to get a lot of nos before you get a yes.

So here's how I look at it: The more nos I get, the closer I'm getting to that yes. I've come to actually appreciate the nos. Sometimes being rejected motivates me even more. It makes me practice more, prepare better, and give it my best shot. I also always try to find out why the company rejected my idea, so I can determine whether it is necessary and possible to improve my presentation or my idea, or both. Ultimately, that feedback improves my chances of eventually getting a yes, or brings me closer to the realization that I need to let the idea go and move on to something else.

With these first calls, that's what's most important: the feedback you get from potential licensees. If your idea or your presentation isn't ready or up to snuff, you need to know. This isn't about getting a pat on the back for coming up with a brilliant idea; it's about licensing your idea and getting it to market, so you can get paid and go find other ideas. When someone tells you no, put your ego and anger aside, and don't try to argue the point. Ask questions why your idea isn't a good fit for the company, and really listen to their answer. Many times, a company has rejected my idea but then given me the keys to the castle by telling me why! I was then able to improve my product and either resubmit it to them or to someone else. Sometimes, the guy who rejects my idea will even direct me to another company.

Every successful entrepreneur on the planet will tell you that rejection is just part of the process; most will tell you that it is a critical part. Mistakes are opportunities to learn and grow. As Soichiro Honda, the late Japanese engineer and founder of Honda Motor Company said, "Success is 99 percent failure."

Don't let fear of rejection keep you from presenting your ideas, and don't take rejection personally. Get that feedback, and keep moving forward.

Fear of Failure

This is the big kahuna of the fears that inhibit product developers. This is the fear that you're going to spend a lot of time and money for nothing, that no one will want your idea, and that it will never see the light of day.

I'm not going to kid you: you will fail. This is a numbers game; to be successful, you need to constantly come up with new ideas. Some will get licensed; others will not. There is no way to guarantee an idea will get licensed. But there is a way to guarantee failure: that is to quit. It would be a crying shame to quit without giving an idea your best shot.

That's what this book is all about: giving you the information and tools to give yourself the best shot at licensing your ideas—*without* breaking your spirit or your bank account. That's why I developed a faster, easier, and cheaper way to bring my ideas to market. The old-school approach of building fancy prototypes and getting patents is just too expensive, time-consuming, and risky. Today, markets change so quickly that by the time you've done all that, not only will you have blown a lot of time and money, but you may also have blown your window of opportunity. In the meantime, someone else may have brought a similar product to market or the market for your idea may have dwindled.

I am living proof that you do not have to spend a lot of money and time to successfully license your ideas. My students are living proof that you don't have to let fear force you to spend a small fortune and years of your life on prototypes and patents. You can find and develop marketable ideas and get them licensed by kicking your fear to the curb and following my road map to bringing an idea to market.

HOW A FEARFUL ROOKIE KNOCKED IT OUT OF THE PARK!

To describe Linda Pollock as shy is an understatement. She is so "painfully shy," she says, "that it hurts." Often, the mere thought of going to a networking event terrorized her to the point that it made her physically sick, giving her an excuse not to go. When she did muster the courage to attend a conference or workshop, she would try to make herself invisible and would leave as soon as the event ended, to avoid talking with anyone. Needless to say, this was not conducive to building a network.

continued

It was at such an event that I met Linda. I happened to be a speaker at that event, and Linda took every word I said to heart. She also purchased the inventRight course, *10 Steps to Bring Your Idea to Market*, and she's taken some of our webinars. You see, her desire to succeed as an inventor was greater than her fear of talking to strangers and failing.

Linda had so many great ideas that she could not decide which one to work on first. I suggested she focus on the one she was most passionate about. Linda is a professional organizer, and she had developed a great idea for a desk organizer. Then she did all the fear-busting, confidence-boosting things I recommend to everyone. She did her homework on potential licensees, created a benefit statement and a sell sheet for her idea, wrote out a cold-call script, and practiced it, practiced it, and practiced it.

Never mind that it then took her three days to "get up the nerve" to make the calls. Never mind that she "fell on [her] face the first time, and the second time, and the third time." Never mind that by the fourth and fifth calls, she was "still spitting out words so fast that I was surprised anyone understood me." What's important is that she made those calls, she articulated her idea and its benefits, they did understand, and she got in the door of many companies.

Then an interesting thing happened: the companies started calling Linda. They asked her questions about her product and her profession. She took that opportunity to ask them questions, too. That's how Linda learned from the experts, licensed her PileSmart idea, and became an expert herself. One company was so impressed with Linda's knowledge that they asked to see more of her ideas *and* hired her to do a presentation of their product line for them. That's how Linda found her voice.

With some knowledge, a few tools, and several successes under her belt, Linda Pollack is no longer afraid of being a fool or failing. When she goes to events, she talks with everybody and is among the last to leave. Picking up the phone and making calls is a breeze. Now, she can open any door and walk right in.

Over the last decade, I have helped thousands of people like Linda kick their fear to the curb and get their ideas into companies. In my experience, I have found that the best offense against fear is information and preparation—and the best defense against fear is information and persistence.

My entire approach to bringing ideas to market is based upon acquiring the information, tools, strategies, and *confidence* you need to get into this game and win it. So kick fear to the curb, get started today, and take it one step at a time.

16

Find the Right Doors to Knock On

MANY PEOPLE get their minds set on licensing their idea to a particular company and don't bother to look any further. Then when that company says no, they put their idea on a shelf. That is a huge mistake, one I have made a couple times early in my career.

The first time I made that goof was with a simple but novel idea: to combine toys with books. For example, I included a box of crayons with a coloring book. I glued the coloring book to a sheet of cardboard that extended about six inches beyond the right edge of the coloring book. Then I glued a plastic tray filled with crayons or colored markers on the cardboard next to the coloring book. My daughter Madeleine loved this idea, and I used a photograph of her demonstrating it on my sell sheet. Other variations included plastic animals that were tied to the story in the book and game pieces for a book of games.

I submitted several variations of my toy-with-book ideas to a company, and they said "no" to every one of them. I did not ask them why, nor did I call any other companies. I just tucked my tail between my legs and put my idea in the reject file.

Today, you can go into any toy store, department store, drug store, or grocery store and find books packaged with toys. I came up with the idea a long time ago, and I can't remember now how much later it was that I saw a book-and-toy product in a store for the first time. What I do know, and what's important for you to know, is that I threw a really good idea away by pitching it to only one company and not even asking for their feedback. Because had I asked them why they said no, chances are I would have realized that my instincts had been right: my idea *was* marketable; it just wasn't right for them. And that would have given me the confidence to find another company to license it.

It only takes a five-minute phone call to find out why a company rejected your idea. Sometimes, the idea is close to what they need, but not quite. If you know what's off (and if you ask, they'll tell you), you can often use that information to tweak your idea and resubmit it to the company or to other companies. Sometimes, it has nothing to do with the merit of your idea. The timing is just wrong. The company may have too many similar items in their product line at that time; but it may be the perfect time for another company.

I didn't realize all that back when I came up with, and prematurely abandoned, my book-and-toy idea. Now that I do know better, I cannot stress enough to you the importance of doing your homework to find as many potential licensees for your idea as possible and of learning as much as you can from them. Because just as you need to come up with many ideas to win this game, so too, do you need to knock on the doors of many companies.

How to Find Potential Licensees

The best way to find potential licensees for your idea is to check out the places where similar products are sold. I do this when I first come up with an idea. I study the marketplace to find out who might buy my product, where they might buy it, and which companies might produce it. Then I design my idea with those consumers, stores, and manufacturers in mind.

Once my idea is ready to submit to companies, I go back and look at the marketplace again, this time to make a list of all the companies that manufacture products similar to mine. That might mean simply reviewing my notes from my earlier market research. Often, it means going back to the local Target or Toys "R" Us or other store to find out which companies have products on the shelves in the aisles where my idea would be. Other times, I might search the Internet or visit the websites of trade associations, trying to find all the major and minor players in a given product category.

A lot of people think that these companies are your competitors. In reality, they are your potential licensees. So find and make a list of all the major players in your product category.

I'VE GOT A SECRET . . .
And I'm going to share it with you. But you're going to have to do a little sleuthing to find it. At inventRight.com, we have a directory of more than 1,300 companies that are looking for ideas. We're adding more companies to the directory all the time. This gold mine of potential licensees is available only to inventRight alumni. But all you have to do to gain access to the directory is visit http://www.inventright.com/links and enter the username *companies* and the password *inventx*.

Zero In on Your Best Bets

After you've identified all the key players in your product category, you'll need to determine which are most likely to be interested in your idea. Back when you were researching whether and how your idea could be manufactured (Chapter 9), you should have uncovered much of the information you'll need now to determine which companies to submit your idea to. But you'll probably have to do a little more homework now. At the very least, check out the company's website and online catalog or store to ensure that your idea fits in with their product lines.

This should go without saying, but I'm going to say it anyway because I'm constantly amazed at how many people fail to do this: only approach companies that have the ability to bring your idea to market. Remember how important it is to know whether your idea will sell and how your idea will be manufactured? It kind of makes me a little crazy when someone calls or sends me an e-mail saying something like, "I tried to pitch my bicycle idea to Radio Shack, and they wouldn't even hear me out. What do I have to do to get in the door?" Well, to begin with, go to another door: to a company that actually makes and sells bikes!

Sometimes people don't do enough homework. They'll find the big players in their general product category but won't look into the range of products they produce within that category. Just because a company produces snack foods doesn't mean they have the ability to produce the frozen snack food idea you've come up with. For example, if they do only dry goods—say, cookies, crackers, chips—they probably don't even have the capacity to do frozen snacks. So of course, they're not going to be interested in your idea. Introducing a whole new product line that requires new manufacturing, distribution, and marketing processes is very expensive and very risky, and companies rarely go that route based on a single idea they've licensed from someone outside the company. Another thing to remember when deciding which companies to call is that size matters.

The biggest companies, the ones that own most of the shelf space, tend to innovate slowly and from within. Although many large corporations do have open-innovation programs, they tend to buy ideas outright rather than license them. That doesn't mean big players don't license ideas from us little guys. Some do, and more are looking outside their walls for fresh ideas all the time. But as a rule of thumb, the biggest doors are the hardest ones to open. On the flip side, small companies often don't have the resources to make and market your idea.

Midsized companies are the most desirable because they have the resources, the need, and the desire to bring new ideas to market. Most midsized companies don't have large in-house R&D departments, so licensing ideas is a more economically feasible way for them to innovate for the market. They're often hungry for ideas that will help them grab a bigger chunk of market share: to go from being the number three to the number two or even the number one player in the market.

I've licensed ideas to companies of all shapes and sizes. So I think it's a good idea to find and get to know all the players in a product category and to not rule out anybody based on size alone. At this point, the only companies you should cross off your list of potential licensees

are the ones that do not sell products similar to yours. But start with the midsized companies first; most of the time, they're your best bet.

When it's time to start pitching a new idea to manufacturers, I always make a list of all the potential licensees and the city in which each is located (the corporate office or headquarters). Sometimes, I make two lists: an A list of my top choices, the companies I think are the best fit for my idea, and a B list of my secondary choices.

Find the Right People to Contact

Many people think they should pitch their ideas to a potential licensee's product development or R&D department. In some companies with open-innovation programs, the product development team may look at ideas from the outside, but they wouldn't be my first choice to cold-call with an idea. Their job is to create new products, and they may not be receptive to someone calling them with a new idea they should have thought of. It makes them look bad.

Contrary to the belief of many inventor types, you should not pitch your idea to someone in engineering or manufacturing, either. Their job is to figure out how to make something *after* marketing and product development have decided they're interested in bringing a new product to market.

Neither do you want to talk with purchasing. Their job is to cut costs and to buy the materials used to manufacture the company's products. They are usually not involved with licensing ideas, other than perhaps to advise management on the availability and cost of materials required to manufacture an idea.

You want to pitch your idea to someone who will understand how your idea benefits the company. You want to get it in front of someone who is going to get excited about your product and say, "This is a great idea! How do we license, manufacture, market, and sell it?" Most of the time, that "right person" is in marketing or sales: a brand manager or director, a marketing manager or director, a sales manager or director, or a product manager.

The best people to pitch your idea to are product managers in the marketing department. Their job is to take an idea from concept to market, and unlike the guys in R&D, they don't care where a good idea comes from. They are also among the hardest people to get a hold of. So if you can't get through to a product manager, your next best bet is someone in sales. Sales reps like to talk and never want to miss a sales lead, so they always answer their phones. If a sales rep or product manager really likes your idea, he or she will pitch it to the marketing manager or marketing director. Then the marketing manager will become your superman. The marketing manager will take ownership of your idea and take it to the vice president or president. So do everything you can think of to get to someone in marketing or sales. They are the ones best able to champion your idea and bring it to market.

Sometimes, when you cold-call a company about an idea, you'll be transferred to the legal department, which is OK but not ideal. In that case, you may be asked to submit your idea to the legal department, and if it passes their muster, they'll pass it along to marketing or product development. But if you can bypass legal and go directly to someone in marketing or sales, that is the better route to go.

The ideal method is to call a company and ask for a product manager or someone else in marketing or sales *by name*. That puts you way ahead of the game. So it pays off to do a little homework to try to find the names of those people on your own.

Some company websites include a directory of key managers, listed by name and job title. The directory may also list the phone number and e-mail of each person; if so, jot them down. But I strongly advise against pitching your idea via e-mail; a phone call is much more effective. You usually want a director or manager—not a president or vice president. High-level executives of big corporations don't look at new ideas; they pass them along to someone farther down the totem pole. At small companies, it may be OK to approach the president or a vice president with your idea, but if there is a lower-level marketing or sales manager, try that person first.

You can also search for marketing and sales professionals at a particular company using one or more of the many business directories and business-networking sites on the Internet. These sites list the addresses, phone numbers, fax numbers, websites, and other pertinent data for companies and business professionals.

Here are a few websites where you can look for the names of a company's marketing and sales managers:

- **LinkedIn,** http://www.linkedin.com: a free, business-oriented social networking site with more than 75 million registered users, spanning more than 200 countries and territories worldwide.
- **Hoovers,** http://www.hoovers.com: a directory database of 65 million companies and more than 85 million professionals, compiled and maintained by a staff of industry experts. Paid subscribers have access to more information and services than do nonsubscribers, but anyone can browse the site by company name, "geography," or industry, and all of the company profiles seem to include a corporate phone number.
- **InfoUSA,** http://infousa.com: InfoGROUP has 12 databases that include contact information for about 14 million businesses in the United States and 1.5 million businesses in Canada. The company verifies this information and updates the database every year.
- **Jigsaw,** http://www.jigsaw.com: an online directory of more than 22 million business professionals from over 3.5 million companies that is compiled, maintained, and accessed by a worldwide community of more than 1 million subscribers.
- **Zoom Info,** http://public.zoominfo.com/search: an online directory that bills itself as "B2B's leading source of business information," where you can search free for information on more than 45 million people and 5 million companies, with 20,000 profiles added daily. You can search the "Companies" database by company name, industry keywords, or location, and the "People" database by the person's name, job title, company name, industry keywords, or city, state, and zip code.
- **XING,** http://www.xing.com: an online networking site for business professionals, similar to LinkedIn but with fewer users (more than 10 million worldwide).

If your homework fails to reveal the name of a product manager, brand manager, sales manager, or some other management-level person in marketing or sales, it at least will have provided you with the phone number of the corporate office. That's where you're most likely to find the right person to whom to pitch your idea.

Sometimes the company's toll-free number will be printed on their products or on the products' packaging. When you're studying the marketplace, it's a good idea to always look for and make note of this phone number—which is usually for customer service. Just call that number and ask customer service for the phone number of the corporate office. For most companies, you can find the main phone number for the corporate office or headquarters by searching online phone directories such as http://www.dexknows.com, http://www.ypyahoo .com, http://www.yellow.com, and http://www.superpages.com. In the U.S. you can also call the directory-assistance number for toll-free numbers: 800-555-1212. Unlike regular directory assistance (411), it's free, and most companies have a toll-free number. You can also track down a company's phone number by searching the Internet using the company's or product name and the word *headquarters* or *corporate* as keywords.

Still another way to find a phone number is to go to the company's official website, where a phone number is often given on a "Contact," "Corporate," or "About" page. Sometimes, you'll visit a company's website and hit pay dirt! For example, I went to Black & Decker's site and clicked on the "Contact Us" page. Bingo! It not only lists the address and a toll-free number for the corporate office, it also has links to the websites of each of the company's brands—organized by product category, no less. Each brand website also has a contact page listing an address and a toll-free number. Not only that, but the corporate website has a "Submit an Idea" page that includes links for submitting ideas!

But I'm getting ahead of myself here. For now, your mission is first to find the right companies to call and if possible, the name of the right person to talk with—and then to get a phone number, any phone number, for each company on your list. Call the number, and follow along until you can speak to a human. It won't be easy, but it's the best way to start from scratch. As for what to say when you make a connection, I'll cover that in the next chapter.

17

The Call That Gets You in the Door

I THINK ONE of the main reasons so many entrepreneurs go to the time, expense, and trouble of making fancy prototypes and getting patents is because they've bought into the myth that "if you build it, they will come." They think the only way to get a big company to say yes is to put on a big show. They think the only way to play with the big boys is to deliver a finished, patented product to their doorstep. It just isn't so.

Prototypes and patents don't open doors, and they don't sell ideas. Preparation and persistence open doors. And benefits kick them wide open.

All the critical steps outlined so far in this book—studying the market, designing for the market, proving your idea, protecting your idea—will help prepare you for the next big step: bringing your idea to market. Now I'm going to show you a simple process for getting a company to say yes to your idea, a process that begins with one of the most basic and most dreaded sales tools: cold-calling.

Why Cold-Calling Is the Best Way to Open Doors

That first phone call—the *cold call,* when you're contacting a complete stranger to tell him or her how your idea can benefit their company—can be intimidating. It is also very important. Although some people use mail or e-mail to introduce their ideas to companies, I have found that the best way to get your foot in the door and your idea licensed is to get someone on the line and build a relationship with that person.

Personally, I think that submitting an idea to a company via e-mail is a bad idea. Many product managers view unsolicited e-mail from strangers as little more than spam, and they may treat it the same way—deleting without even reading it. If the company's website has an online form or e-mail link for submitting ideas, you're more likely to get your idea in front of the right person that way than with a regular e-mail. But you'll still want to call to make sure the person received your idea and to get his or her feedback on it.

Even if a company does have an online form for submitting ideas, I still think it is more effective to call first, for several reasons:

1. You are more likely to get your idea to the right person with a phone call than with an e-mail, and you'll at least know that he or she is actually aware of your idea.
2. Your confidence in and passion for your idea are more likely to come through your voice than through your writing.
3. The product manager is more likely to ask you any questions he or she might have while you are on the phone than in a responding e-mail.
4. You can usually gauge a company's interest in your idea during that first phone call. When you submit an idea via e-mail, you will probably receive a form e-mail that essentially says, "Thanks for the idea. We'll call you if we're interested," after which you'll wait weeks or months for their real take on your idea, if they ever contact you again at all.
5. If the product manager says no to your idea, you can immediately ask why. You can also ask whether the product manager can recommend another company who might be interested. It is much more difficult to get this type of feedback via e-mail, and you are unlikely to get it as quickly as with a phone call.
6. You can offer to send your sell sheet during your phone conversation, and if the product manager agrees, you can send or fax him or her your sell sheet immediately.

I'm not saying e-mail and mail never work. I'm just saying that cold-calling has worked much better for me and my students.

I'm also not saying that cold-calling always gets you to the right person quickly and easily, or even that it always get you in the front door. Sometimes you have to go through other doors, and often you have to make several calls before you get your idea to the right person. But cold-calling is a lot easier than you might think, when you follow my simple approach to contacting potential licensees.

The Right Way to Cold-Call

In an ideal world, you would have the name of a product manager *and* his or her direct line or extension number before you place the call, *and* the person you need to speak with would answer your first call. More often, you have to call a company's general number and go through one or more gatekeepers to find the right person to review your idea. Then you have to make several more calls before that person actually answers the phone or takes your call. No wonder cold-calling is so nerve-wracking and frustrating to so many people!

You can make cold-calling a lot easier and more effective by following these simple strategies.

Prepare a Script and Practice, Practice, Practice

Whenever it's time to start pitching an idea to potential licensees, I always type what I'm going to say on an index card. I practice reading the script out loud over and over again, and then I practice it with my wife or one of my kids until it feels and sounds right.

I always start by saying who I am and the purpose of my call, and I usually include some version of that magic word "help" in my opening statement:

> *Hi, my name is Stephen Key. I'm a product developer, and I need a little help. I have a great new product I would like to submit to your company. Who could I speak with?*

If the operator says something like, "I don't know who handles that," or "I'll transfer you to purchasing (or some other inappropriate department)," I'll say something like, "Maybe I could speak to someone in marketing or sales," or "Is there someone in marketing who deals with hand tools?"

Sometimes, an operator will tell me the name and title of the person to whom he or she is about to transfer the call: "Certainly. I'll connect you with Sheila Sanders. She's the director of marketing." If that happens, quickly jot down this information. If you have time, ask the operator for the person's extension or direct line. That way, you can bypass the operator the next time you call.

If the operator says only, "Certainly. I'll transfer you now," try to ask for the name, title, and extension of the person to whom the operator is forwarding your call. If you're prepared to ask, you may be able to get this information before the operator gets off the line.

If all the stars are aligned and the operator gives you the name of the person he or she's transferring you to and that person answers the phone, start off by greeting him or her by name. Say who you are and the purpose of your call—this time giving the type of product you've developed and its big benefit. (Remember your benefit statement?) Then offer to send additional information:

> *Hello, Ms. Sanders. My name is Stephen Key. I'm a product developer, and I have an innovative new label that adds 75 percent more space for information to your containers. Can I send you additional information?*

Write a script that covers all of these possible scenarios, and then practice it by role-playing with a family member or friend. Once you've nailed your cold-calling script, start calling companies.

Call the Last Company on Your List First

With cold-calling, as with most things, practice makes perfect. The first calls you make will probably feel awkward, and you'll probably fumble a few. So use the one or two companies that are least likely to license your idea or that you're the least excited about licensing your idea as trial runs. Then work your way up your list, so that the third, fifth, or tenth call is to the company you most want to license your idea.

Even after you have some cold-calling experience under your belt, you may find that the first couple calls of the day go less smoothly than those you make once you've warmed up a bit. After years of cold-calling, I still sometimes fumble my first calls of the day. So again, I start off my morning by making the least important calls, and if I trip up, I try to recover as quickly and gracefully as possible. I've also learned to just laugh at myself. Once in a while I'll bumble a call so badly that I'll chuckle and say, "Hey, can I start over?" No one has ever said no.

Never Call Yourself an Inventor

The word "inventor" has negative connotations for many people. They immediately envision a hermit with thick glasses, wild hair, and a pocket protector stuffed with pens, who tinkers with weird stuff in his shed or basement and never talks to his neighbors. To marketing and salespeople—the folks you want to talk with—the word "inventor" often means someone who is out of touch with the market and builds complex prototypes and files patents on stuff nobody wants.

So never introduce yourself as an inventor. Instead, say that you are a "product developer" or give the name of your "design" company:

Hi, my name is Stephen Key. I'm a product developer, or *Hi, I'm Stephen Key with Stephen Key Design.*

The words "product developer" and "design" both imply that I'm developing products for the market, not for my own curiosity. These terms convey legitimacy, and they are words marketing, sales, and R&D people commonly use themselves.

Stay Focused on the Call

When you're calling potential licensees, you want to be in a quiet place and focused solely on making calls, not doing or thinking about anything else. If you're on the phone and something, someone, or some thought distracts you, you're more likely to blow your pitch: to speak too fast, ramble, garble your one-line benefit statement, not offer to send additional information, or make some other goof. If a potential licensee hears your radio, television, coworkers, family, or some other background noise, like people talking in a café, it could signal to them that you're not very professional, and then they may not give your idea the consideration it deserves.

Call at the Right Time

The best days to call a busy professional are Tuesday, Wednesday, and Thursday. On Monday, most people are figuring out their schedule for the week and focusing on their own goals. On Friday, they're trying to wrap up the workweek and get out of the office to begin their weekend.

The best times to call are just before 8:00 A.M., just after 1:00 P.M. (lunchtime), and just after 5:00 P.M., their time, when the product manager, rather than a secretary, is more likely to answer the phone. Of course, you can and should call anytime during regular business hours, but if you're having trouble reaching someone, try calling 10 minutes before the office workday begins, 10 minutes after lunch, or 10 minutes before the workday ends, when managers are more likely to answer their own phones.

I once mentioned to my wife that I could get through to anyone within any company. At the time, Janice was the VP of marketing at E&J Gallo Winery, and she said, "There is no way you could get to me." She knew her gatekeepers, the operator and her secretary, would screen all her calls. But I knew that my wife, like other people who are climbing the corporate ladder and trying to get ahead, would always be at her desk before the gatekeepers arrived and after they had gone home. And she would pick up the phone at those times, just in case it was her boss or another higher-up in the company. Guess what? I got through!

Of course, in today's age of caller ID, the people you're trying to reach may just ignore a phone number they don't recognize and let your call go to voice mail—no matter when or how many times you call. In that case, you'll have no choice but to leave a message, so make sure you leave the *right* one, such as the example I provide in the next section.

Speaking of caller ID: make sure to unblock your phone, or make it a practice to answer incoming calls whenever possible. The person you've been trying to reach may call from a different number than the one you called, and you don't want to miss a call from a potential licensee.

Leave the Right Message and Only as a Last Resort

A lot of people disagree with me on this, but I'm adamant about it. When I'm cold-calling someone to pitch my idea, I try not to leave a voice message. I just keep calling back until I make contact, and I look for other ways to get in the door.

The only time I leave a message is after I've tried four or five times with no success. Then I leave a message that goes something like this:

> *Hi! This is Stephen Key; I'm a product developer, and I'd like to show you a label that gives you 75 percent more space for information. You can reach me at 1-800-701-7993. If I don't hear back from you, I'll just keep trying.*

If my one-line benefit statement doesn't motivate them to call me back, that last line does. It tells them that I am persistent and will keep trying.

Call Several Companies

The more companies you have looking at your idea, the more likely you are to get a hit. I always submit my ideas to at least two or three and often four or more companies. If I had showed my ideas to one company at a time, there is no way I would be as successful as I have been. Licensing is a numbers game; to succeed, you have to submit a lot of ideas to a lot of companies.

Companies do not expect you to submit your idea exclusively to them. Very rarely are two companies interested in an idea at the same time, and if they are, that's a good problem to have! Not only does it give you the option of choosing the best licensee for your idea, it also gives you leverage to cut a great licensing deal.

Call More than One Person Within a Company

If you can't get through to a particular person, try calling someone else in the company. If you can't get through to someone in marketing, try another department: sales, brand management, product development, R&D. If one person says he or she's not interested in seeing your idea, try someone else. Just because a product manager doesn't want to see your idea doesn't mean someone in sales won't. Likewise, while marketing and sales tend to be more receptive to "outside" ideas than product development and R&D are, that may not be the case at the company you're trying to get into. Your idea may be exactly what they're looking for, but the only way they'll know that is if you call and tell them. The best way for you to get your idea licensed is to cast a wide net, pitching it to as many receptive ears as possible.

By knocking on several doors within a company, I've been able to get at least one of them to open and to get someone to look at my ideas. You can too!

Be Persistent

Some companies are huge, and you may run into a few obstacles and may need to call numerous times before you get through to someone who actually takes your call. Other companies won't know how to handle your call either, because they don't have "official" open-innovation programs or because they get few, if any, calls from independent product developers. Most people don't realize they can license their ideas to companies, and so most companies get few, if any, calls from people like you and me.

Regardless of a company's program, or lack of, for reviewing outside ideas, one of the most common obstacles to get past are the gatekeepers: the operator who answers the company's main number, an assistant who directs all calls for a particular department, or an assistant to the person you're trying to reach. An operator may be unaware the company even looks at outside ideas for products, and assistants may be unfamiliar with the company's open-innovation policies or may simply be overly focused on running interference for their boss. That is why it is to your advantage to get the name and the direct line of the person you want to reach, which increases the odds that they, rather than a gatekeeper, will answer the call.

Once you get the name of a product manager, or any other name, keep calling until you connect with that person. These people are busy; it could take several calls—a dozen calls!—before you get them on the line. Remember, don't leave a voice message; try calling 10 minutes before and 10 minutes after the company's office hours. Keep calling until you get to actually talk with the person you're trying to reach. Be persistent.

Every once in a while you will call a company and a gatekeeper will tell you the company does not take outside submissions. Just because the gatekeeper says so doesn't make it so. For most companies, calls from product developers wanting to submit their ideas are few and far between. The operator may simply be unaware that the company has an open-innovation policy. The secretary may just be overprotective, trying to do his or her job. Your job is to get around the gatekeepers to someone who is involved with marketing, selling, or developing new products. Those are the only people who can really say whether your idea is a possible fit for their company.

One of our inventRight graduates called one day to tell me about how he had called a company, delivered his "fast pitch" to the operator, and was told the company did not take outside submissions. But he followed my advice. He was persistent. He called back about an hour later and asked if he could speak to someone in sales. That's all he said: "Can I speak to someone in sales?" When the sales rep came on the line, he introduced himself, rattled off his one-line benefit statement, and asked if he could send him some additional information. "Sure," the sales rep said. "Send me more info on that. It sounds interesting!"

Sometimes you need to be creative to get around roadblocks. And you always need to be persistent.

Speak with Confidence and Enthusiasm

I have found that how you speak is almost as important as what you say. If you have a positive attitude and are passionate about your idea, it will come through in your voice. Likewise, if you're feeling down or insecure, that will come through over the phone, too. After all, the person on the other end of the phone can't see you or read your body language; he or she can only listen to the tone of your voice and your words. If you don't seem confident and enthusiastic about your idea, how can you expect someone else to be?

So first of all, believe in your idea. Because you've done your homework, you can be confident that you've innovated for the market, your product can be manufactured, and it will sell. Practicing your pitch will also help you gain confidence and get more comfortable with cold-calling. Then do whatever else helps you put yourself in a positive and professional frame of mind. If that means making calls in your pajamas, do that. If it means putting on business clothes and going to your private office, do that. If you feel more energized and clearheaded when you stand, then stand up when you're talking with someone. And smile. That's what I do: when I call a potential licensee, I'm feeling good, I'm dressed, I'm standing up, I'm excited about my idea, and I'm smiling. All that confidence and enthusiasm carries right through the telephone line to that other person.

Keep It Short and Focused on Benefits

The purpose of a cold call is to get your foot in the door. That's it. The person you're calling—out of the blue, as far as he's concerned—doesn't want to hear a detailed description of your idea. He doesn't want to know how it works and how it's manufactured. He doesn't want to hear some sales spiel. And he sure as heck doesn't want to hear that it's the hottest, most innovative, most perfect product for his company ever. He wouldn't even absorb all of that, given that people remember only about 7 percent of what they hear. But he isn't going to give you time to say all of that, anyway. You're going to have a minute or two to say the only things he wants to know: *Who are you? Why are you calling me? What's in it for me?*

The only thing he really wants to know, in 60 seconds or less, is how your idea will benefit his company—and make him look like a hero. So use those 60 seconds wisely: Introduce yourself. Give your one-line benefit statement. Offer to send additional information. Thank him for his time and consideration. Then hang up and move on to the next call on your list.

On those rare occasions when the person tries to get you to talk about your idea at length during that first call, don't do it. Instead, tell her that the literature you're sending will explain the benefits of your idea, and then politely end the call.

Take Notes

Keep a detailed record of all your calls. This log can be on paper or in the computer, and it should include the person's name, the company's name, the date of the call, and a note summarizing the call itself. It is very important to keep track of everyone you've pitched your idea to, what you said to that person, and that person's response.

Ask to Send Additional Information

Unless you're told that the company does not accept outside ideas, end every cold call by asking if you can send additional information. Send your sell sheet, drawing, video, or other information *only* if you get the green light to do so.

Before you start calling companies, make sure to have a supply of sell sheets (and whatever other information you wish to send) ready to go. That way, if the product manager or salesperson wants to review your idea, you can send off the information immediately.

Always include a one-page submission letter printed on your business letterhead and your business card. I suggest creating a boilerplate submission letter and saving it to your computer; then when you need to send the letter, you can just personalize the letter with the company name, the person's name and mailing address, and the date. Make sure the letter includes a one-sentence description of your idea that highlights its big benefit, and add a note reminding the person of when you contacted him or her, that the person agreed to review your idea, and any other important details of your phone conversation.

Make sure to get this package out the same day or the day after your phone call, and use second-day or third-day delivery. If you're sending only a submission letter and sell sheet, sometimes you can fax them.

One other tip: I never ask the person for his or her address or fax number, because the person's time is at a premium. Instead, I call the operator or the department secretary afterward to get a mailing address or fax number.

Be Patient

Getting your foot in the door is only the first step in what is often a long process. It usually takes a while—weeks, if not months—for a company to review your idea to see whether it's a potential fit for their customers and operations. So be patient, and don't hound your contact with phone calls and e-mails asking, "What's up?"

Give your package of information enough time to arrive; then call or e-mail to confirm that it has. Take this opportunity to ask your contact how the process will work and when to expect a decision. Then make a note to follow up a few days beyond that target date, in the event you don't hear back from the person by that time.

While you're waiting for the company to go through their review process, don't just sit by the phone waiting for their call. Instead, pick it up and call other companies. If you've called all the companies on your list, start working on another idea.

If you don't hear back from a company that is reviewing your idea within a reasonable period of time, it's OK to call your main contact to check on the status of things. This is also a good time to ask whether the person has any questions and whether you can provide him or her with any additional information to help with the review process.

If You Get a No, Get Feedback

When you finally get an answer from the company, it will come in one of two forms: a letter or a phone call. If it's a yes, congratulations! It's time to move on to the contract negotiation part of the licensing process, which I'll cover in the next chapter.

If the answer is no, you will get the disappointing news in one of two ways: a phone call or a letter. It is hard to hear "no" over the phone, regardless of whether you placed or received the call. Take a deep breath, and take this opportunity to ask why the company is not interested in your idea. If you receive a rejection letter, take a few minutes to call your contact to thank the person for letting you know that your idea isn't a fit for the company and then politely ask why. Most of the time, the person will gladly give you an honest and short answer. Maybe it's just the wrong time. Maybe the price point is too high. Maybe your idea is right for the market but not right for the company in question. Sometimes, you can use this feedback to change your idea to fit the market, or simply take your idea to a different company. For example, after learning that a toy idea of mine had been rejected because the company's product line had too many toys in that category, I was able to license it to a different manufacturer.

How Tom Licensed His Idea in Two Weeks

One of our inventRight students sent me an e-mail recently telling me that after cold-calling four or five companies using my method, he was "amazed at how easy it was to get into companies and pitch my ideas!" He also reported that in the eight months since then, his "fear of making cold calls has vanished."

Once he started making those calls, Tom licensed his first product in less than two weeks. Although he had to call multiple companies before he finally got one to say yes to reviewing his idea, that company, Sportcraft, licensed his idea after the sales team got excited after watching Tom's YouTube video demonstrating his product, the Disclub.

In the beginning, Tom would write out a script, practice it, change it a couple times, practice it some more, and then pick up the phone. Now, "the script is long gone," his confidence has soared, he's having "a blast" calling companies, and he's "on the way" to his next licensing deal.

Slip in Through the Back Door

Sometimes it is impossible to get in through the front door, especially with large corporations like Coca-Cola and Procter & Gamble. At best, it is difficult, and you often end up with the legal department. That's not necessarily a bad thing, but it takes longer and is more complicated, and if they say no to your idea, you usually can't find out why.

When the sentries at the front door are keeping you away from the people in marketing and sales you need to talk with, you need to be creative and find other doors to knock on.

Following are some other ways to get your foot in the door.

Think out of the Box

There will be times when you just can't get through to anyone in marketing or sales. Do a little brainstorming to try to think of some other department or person in the company who might be interested in your idea. For example, when I was getting nowhere by asking for someone in marketing and sales at McNeil (makers of Tylenol and other consumer health care products) to pitch my rotating label idea, I was able to get in touch with someone in the design department who worked on graphics for labels.

Network Your Way In

Do you know someone who knows someone at the company? It doesn't even have to be as direct a connection as that; the chain can be several "someones" long. You just need this connection to allow you to use his or her name when you call this contact within the company—or better yet, to refer you directly to that person. This is how I got into Procter & Gamble; the father of a friend of mine showed a crude prototype of my rotating label idea to the CEO of P&G while playing golf with him. Although that didn't result in a licensing deal with P&G, it led me to build a wall of patents around my idea; now other companies have licensed and sold more than 400 million of my Spinformation label.

Start at the Local Level

If you can't get through the front door of the corporate office, call a regional sales manager, branch manager, or franchise owner and try to get that person interested in your idea. For example, I couldn't get through to anyone at PepsiCo headquarters to pitch my rotating label idea, so I got in contact with a local Pepsi bottling franchise owner. He liked my idea, and he was able to take it to some top executives at Pepsi and get them interested in it, too.

Knock on Their Ad Agency's Door

All big corporations have advertising agencies who brag about their clients to help attract new business. You can find the ad agency for any company by going to the agency's website, doing an Internet search (e.g., "Pepsi ad agency"), or browsing *Advertising Age* online (http://www.adage.com). Call and ask to speak with the account manager of the company you want to submit your idea to; don't tell the operator why you're calling, only that you'd like to speak to the account manager. You'll usually be put right through, because the assumption is you're a potential new client and they're always looking for new business. Tell the account exec you have a product innovation one of their clients might be interested in. If he or she bites, show your idea (one-line benefit statement and sell sheet). It doesn't always work, but once in a while it does.

This is exactly how I got into Coca-Cola. I knew that Primo Angeli, a large design studio in San Francisco (not far from where we live) had their advertising account because the agency also represented E&J Gallo Winery, where my wife worked. I called them about my rotating label, and because they were close, I went there to meet with them. I showed them some samples, including a Coke bottle with my spinning label on it. They picked it up, spun it, and told me they'd be back in a minute. Five minutes later, the agency owner, Primo Angeli, walked into the room and asked, "Do you mind if we show this to our client?"

Sure enough, I got a call from Coca-Cola, and the next thing I knew, I was in Atlanta meeting with them. Although I did not get a contract at that time, the feedback I got at that meeting led me to redesign my label so it could be manufactured faster and at a lower cost. That enabled me to license my Spinformation label to Coca-Cola in Mexico as well as to Accudial and others.

Try Pull-Through Marketing

Pull-through marketing is when you get the company's customers—the businesses that sell their products to consumers—interested in your idea and then they tell the company's sales and marketing people about it. One way to get your idea in front of a company's customers is to show it to buyers and distributors at trade shows. Another way is to call a buyer at Target, Home Depot, PetSmart, or whatever other major retailer sells the company's products to see if they're interested in your idea. When a big customer tells a company, "Hey, I like this idea," the company will usually open the door and invite you in to show them your idea.

If you were to ask a group of product developers whose ideas never made it to market why they did not, nine out of ten will tell you it's because they were unable to get their idea in to the manufacturers. If you were to ask what they did to try to get their ideas to manufacturers, you would learn that they made some of the simple mistakes you learned about in this chapter, like sending e-mails and letters without calling first, introducing themselves as an inventor, leaving voice mail messages, rambling and stumbling over their own words on the phone, calling the wrong companies, talking to the wrong people, not articulating the benefit of their idea, not being prepared and not being persistent.

But when you use the simple strategies and tools outlined in this chapter, doors open. When you call the right people at the right companies and say the right things, someone will let you in to show them your idea. Every week one of my students calls or e-mails to tell me they got into three, four, or more companies. They are often shocked at how easy it is to get in using this approach. I'm not. I know it works. I also know that the more you do it, the easier and more effective it becomes.

PART SEVEN

Bring Your Ideas to Market

You've come up with a marketable idea, validated and protected it, researched potential licensees, and found the courage to call them. As a result, you've accomplished something many entrepreneurial product developers only dream of: you got the right people at the right companies to look at your idea. Now one or more of those companies has expressed interest in licensing it.

You're so excited and nervous, your head is spinning! *What royalty percentage will I get? When do I get paid? What about patents? What if they want an exclusive? Do I have any say in what happens to my idea once they license it? Should I arrange a meeting with the company? Should I call an attorney? What should I do next?*

First, take a deep breath or a long walk. Relax. Negotiating a licensing agreement takes a clear head and a good amount of time, but playing with the big boys is actually easier than you might think. All it takes is information and a few simple strategies. Let me show you the right way to cut a great deal, get your ideas to market, and live the licensing lifestyle.

Cut a Great Deal

THE CONVENTIONAL way to negotiate a licensing agreement is to hire an attorney to do it for you. As you may have guessed by now, I only follow convention when it's the best way to get me to where I want to go. If I can find a faster, easier, and cheaper route, I take it. And I have found that doing my own negotiating puts me way ahead of the game.

I actually like to negotiate my own deals, but I also like that it saves me money in attorney fees. Now I'm not suggesting that you negotiate a licensing contract without legal advice. I'm suggesting that you be the go-to person in all direct dealings with a potential licensee. Once you and the company have ironed out any issues and agreed on the main terms of the agreement, then it's time to bring in the attorneys.

Cutting a licensing deal is a lot like playing tennis. Various issues get lobbed back and forth until an agreement is reached. Just when you think all the issues have been resolved, you realize you've only played the first game of the first set and there is another whole match to go. If your attorney is playing for you, the costs add up quickly. Doing the negotiating yourself saves you money. It also usually makes the process go smoother and faster.

Another reason I prefer to do my own negotiating is that it enables me to better understand the potential licensee's business and to develop a relationship with a key player inside the company. As a result, any problems with the contract can be resolved more efficiently, and the deal we end up with is more likely to provide optimal benefits to both the company and me. It then helps me ensure my product is brought to market and my royalties are paid promptly and properly. It also gives me an advantage if I want to license another idea to the company later.

Cutting a great deal is all about knowing what a potential licensee wants and what you want, and then working together as a team to hammer out a win-win agreement. This usually takes time, anywhere from six weeks to six months. It also takes information—the most powerful tool you can bring to any bargaining table.

Leveling the Playing Field

Going up against a big company can be intimidating. They have a whole team of seasoned experts on their side, and it's just you and your attorney, which I've just advised you to hold off bringing in until the ninth inning. The manufacturer is going to come to the bargaining table with a game plan, and they're going to ask you a lot of questions. One of the first questions they'll ask is, "What do you want?" Regardless of how you answer, they're probably going to want to give you less.

I level the playing field by coming to the bargaining table:

- Having a good idea of what I want and of what the company might want
- With a good understanding of the company and their market
- Prepared to ask my own questions
- With the attitude that we are on the same team, rather than opposing teams, and that together we can work out a win-win agreement

I start preparing for the contract-negotiation process *before* I get the call from a potential licensee saying, "We're interested in your idea." While they're reviewing my idea, I find out what they sell, how much they sell, and where they sell it.

Let's say a beverage company is reviewing my Spinformation label. Before we start negotiating a licensing agreement, I would want to know all the different product categories they produce. Do they sell soft drinks, energy drinks, bottled water, juice, tea, milk, beer, wine, hard liquor? Which national and international territories do they cover? Are their products sold by big-box retail stores, convenience stores, specialty stores? Do they sell to commercial accounts? How many units of each product category do they sell annually?

You should have some of this information already, from when you were studying the market, finding out how to manufacture your idea, and looking for potential licensees. But you'll probably need to do more in-depth research now to find out what, where, and how much the company sells.

Here are a few ways to find this kind of information:

- **Ask people.** Call a sales rep at another company in the same industry, or call an industry expert, perhaps at a trade association. Ask about sales of a certain product industrywide, the market strength of the company you're researching, and where their products sell well and don't sell well, and so on. You can even call a sales rep within the company, tell him or her you're writing a business plan or a paper for a class, and ask about their different product categories (brands), sales territories, and sales volumes.
- **Visit the company's website.** You can usually find product information and something about even sales figures on the website's "About," "Corporate," "Products," "Brand," "Annual Report," or other pages. For example, the "About" Web page of Kraft Foods says the company sells in more than 160 countries and has more than 80 brands; it also gives product and market information for each brand.
- **Browse trade publications and trade association websites.** Look for articles, press releases, reports, and announcements on market data and stats for the industry, a product category, or a particular company.
- **Check online business directories.** These websites feature company profiles that sometimes include the information you're looking for. Several online directories are listed in Chapter 17, but

there are hundreds more: some focused on a particular industry, industry segment, product category, or geographic area; others are worldwide directories of a wide range of companies.

- **Search the Internet.** For example, when I search the keywords "Coca-Cola sales distribution 2009," I got more than 80,000 results, including an Answers.com page stating the corporation markets "3,000 drinks under 500 brand names in some 200 nations" and citing the company's major brands, the location of each of its principal divisions, and its principal competitors.

You may not be able to find all the sales information you need. That's OK; you can ask the company for it later. What's important is that you have an understanding of a potential licensee's operations, products, and markets before you start negotiating a licensing deal with them.

Negotiating a Win-Win Licensing Agreement

When a company is considering licensing your idea, they will often ask what you need, in terms of money, to make it happen. Sometimes they'll throw out a base offer: for example, worldwide exclusive, three to five percent (royalty), five years.

I've been doing this for years and have had hundreds of companies interested in my ideas, and I still get a rush whenever I find out a company is interested in my idea. It's a great feeling! It can make you want to jump up and down and shout, "Yes! I'll take it! Where do I sign?" Go ahead and jump up and down, but don't say yes to anything and don't get too excited this early in the game.

Just because a company is interested in your idea doesn't mean you'll end up with a licensing contract. Deals fall out all the time. Don't expect to cut a deal right away, either. Licensing deals take time and a lot of negotiating. Although you may be the sole decision maker on your end, several people and departments are typically involved in licensing decisions on the company's end. I used to want to resolve everything in one conversation. Now I know that it may take several calls, lots of correspondence, and many weeks or months to work out an agreement. So I have learned to relax and be patient, and I try to approach the process as a team player and a problem solver.

Actually, when I get that first phone call or e-mail saying, "Stephen, we're interested in your idea. How can we move forward?" I like to slow down the process. This is an ideal time to ask important questions that will help me negotiate the best deal possible. So I usually respond by asking, "Do you want an exclusive or a nonexclusive?"

Exclusive means the potential licensee wants to prohibit other companies from manufacturing and marketing your product. If the company wants exclusive rights, and most do, it is very important to define the parameters of this exclusivity. So the next thing I ask is for which territory or territories they want an exclusive. If the company has more than one category or brand in which my product might fit (which I already know through my research), I also ask for which product categories or brands they want an exclusive.

Early in the process, I also ask for sales information. I want to know the most recent sales volume of each product category in which my product will be sold. I want to know the company's sales projections for my product, broken down by sales territory, if possible. I also want to know the wholesale price they intend to charge for my product.

If the company is reluctant to give you this or any other information you ask for, explain that you just want to understand their business and how they intend to use your idea. If they still won't give you the information, then tell them you'll get back with them shortly and go research it yourself. But most companies will be forthcoming with this information, because they need it too and for the same reason you do: to determine the best possible terms of the licensing agreement.

Take good notes of all your research and of every conversation with a potential licensee, and make sure to keep every piece of correspondence you send and receive from them. Chances are, you will need to go back and forth several times before all of your questions and theirs get answered and before you come to agreement on all terms.

Now let's take a closer look at how to address some of the most critical terms of a licensing agreement.

Exclusive Rights

Most companies will want a worldwide exclusive guaranteeing that only they can manufacture and sell your idea. That's a good thing. You want an exclusive. An exclusive has a high value! But you should always ask the person you're negotiating with to define what is meant by *exclusive*.

From your earlier research, you may have learned that a potential licensee has strong sales in certain countries, isn't strong in others, and doesn't sell at all in others. It might be to your advantage to break the licensing deal into different geographic territories, with the company paying more for exclusive rights in their main territories, less for nonexclusive rights in their secondary territories, and reserving no rights in territories where they have no plans to sell your product. For example, the company may want exclusives in the United States, Canada, and Mexico, each of which is a huge market. However, the company sells very little in Mexico, where two or more other companies dominate the market. So rather than lumping all three countries into one licensing deal, you could negotiate an exclusive for only the United States and Canada. That way, you would have the option of licensing your idea to a different company with strong marketing and distribution in Mexico.

The same goes for product categories: your idea may be suitable for categories in which the manufacturer does not sell products. That's why I usually ask, "For which categories do you want an exclusive?" to which the company usually responds, "What do you mean by categories?"

Let's say I'm negotiating with a soda company to license my rotating label and the company says, "We want your label for all beverages." I would have to say, "Well, let's talk about that." The beverage industry is huge and includes several product categories.

If the soda manufacturer sells mostly soft drinks, water, and juice and only in the United States, Canada, and Mexico, I could offer them exclusive rights for those three product categories and in those three territories. If the company were coming out with a new energy drink and had recently acquired a large beer producer in Japan, they could counter that they want exclusives in those product categories and in that territory as well.

You may also want to further define *exclusive* by sales channel. Does the company want to sell your product in only big-box retail stores like Target, Home Depot, Toys "R" Us, Walmart, and Costco? Do they want to sell your product in drugstores and supermarkets, too? What about convenience stores and specialty stores? What about institutional sales, such as hospitals, hotels, restaurants, schools, and the military? Maybe the company would be willing to limit their exclusivity to only major retailers and food service providers.

Will a company always agree to restrict their exclusive rights? Will holding back some markets work in your favor? Is there a substantial global market for your idea? I can't answer that, because every company, every product, and every deal is different. The only way to find out is to do your homework, discuss exclusives with the company, and decide what is in your best interests. Maybe the only way a company will license your idea is if you give them a worldwide exclusive. Maybe it's the only game in town, and no other company will be interested in licensing your idea. Maybe no one will want to take a chance on your idea outside the United States, and that's OK. The U.S. market is plenty big for most products. Whether the company wants an exclusive on all or some markets, you should be compensated properly for the rights they are licensing.

Remember, the company isn't buying your idea outright. They're renting the right to manufacture and market your product for a specific market, a specific period of time, and a specific rate of compensation. Each piece of an exclusive has value, and you need to be adequately compensated for it. You can give away some value, but you can and should keep some value for yourself. One strategy I sometimes use is to hold back on certain countries the company wants and then later offer to give them those territories if they're willing to pay for the patents in those countries.

Here's another negotiating strategy that my students and I have had success with: Let's say a potential licensee wants worldwide retail rights to your idea but sells only to Walgreens drugstores. You could say something like, "I will give you an exclusive for all retail categories, even though you sell only in Walgreens." This lets the company know you are making a concession, that it's not a perfect deal for you, but it gives you some leverage in negotiating a higher royalty and higher minimum guarantees.

Royalty

A royalty is a percentage of the wholesale sales of your product. Companies pay licensing royalties four times a year, once per fiscal quarter based on the previous fiscal quarter. Each payment is due and payable within 30 days of the last day of the fiscal quarter. For example, if the first quarter is January through March, the first-quarter royalty check would be due and payable by April 30.

People often ask me, "What is a fair royalty rate?" What's fair is whatever you can get—or the most you can get! I know that sounds terrible, but it is reality. Royalty rates vary somewhat from industry to industry. So find out the average royalty rate in your industry; a trade association or someone who has successfully licensed ideas in that product category or industry should be able to provide you with this information.

I know of many entrepreneurs who have killed deals by asking for an unreasonable royalty. As a rule of thumb, 10 percent is too high and 1 percent is too low, though it depends on the product, the company, and the market. For most ideas, five to seven percent is a fair royalty rate. What I usually do is start at seven percent, and it usually works its way down to five percent.

Some ideas warrant a larger royalty. Of course, there are the big ideas owned by the Disneys of the world, but there are also situations in which a small idea can command a higher royalty rate. For example, if the company is going to sell a relatively small amount of your product and the profit margins are high enough, you might want to ask for 10 percent and settle for no less than 8 percent. The novelty business is like that sometimes. For example, they'll license your idea for a few months during the Christmas season or some other shopping season (e.g., summer). They may license a seasonal product for a single season or for a few seasons.

Sometimes, a smaller royalty is in order: for example, if your patent doesn't issue or no intellectual-property protection is available in that country or if sales volumes are very large. If my Spinformation label were on a beverage that sold billions of units a day, the licensing royalty could be a fraction of a percent. Your royalty percentage will also be less if you need to split it with someone else. For instance, I received a smaller royalty for the Michael Jordan Wall Ball because the royalty was shared between me and Michael Jordan.

Ultimately, the right royalty is the rate you're able to negotiate. Just be careful not to give away your idea for less than it is worth, and don't dig in your heels on a royalty that is deal-breakingly high.

Advance Against Royalties

Asking for a big lump-sum payment upfront is the number one way entrepreneurs and independent product developers kill a deal. This is called "top-loading" a licensing agreement, and it's a lousy way to do business. It does not take into consideration the manufacturer's situation, signaling to a potential licensee that you are looking out only for yourself and aren't all that interested in reaching a win-win agreement. It doesn't exactly foster the kind of mutually respectful and beneficial long-term partnership that you want, or should want, to establish with the manufacturer that is going to be selling your product for years to come . . . and maybe license another of your ideas in the future.

Typically, though, some sort of money needs to be paid upfront as a gesture of goodwill. Most potential licensees will agree to pay a small advance. However, they will not offer it, so you will need to ask for it.

Here is what I like to do: in lieu of a big advance, I ask the manufacturer to pay for my patents. In fact, that is how I've paid for all of my patents. My attorneys filed them and I own them, but my licensees paid for them. While an advance is a gesture of goodwill, having a company pay for your patents is good business. It protects the company's interests as well as yours, and it helps incent and motivate the licensee to bring your idea to market so they can recoup the patent costs.

Sometimes, the manufacturer will be willing to pay a small cash advance in addition to paying for your patents. It all depends on how big your idea is and how much money they stand to make.

Minimum Guarantees

One of the most powerful bargaining chips you can use is something called "minimum guarantees," which on a licensing contract is a type of "performance clause." The minimum guarantee in a licensing agreement specifies the minimum amount of money (a dollar amount) the company will pay you the first year (or quarter), the second year, the third year, and so on, regardless of how much of your product the licensee actually sells. If they sell more than projected, you will receive more than the minimum guarantee for that year. If they sell less, you still get paid the minimum guaranteed amount for that year. If they do not pay the minimum guarantee, you get back the licensing rights to your product.

Without some sort of performance clause, the licensee could sit on your idea forever and never pay you, and you could be prevented from licensing your idea to another company. With minimum guarantees, if the licensee fails to bring your idea to market, you have the right to cancel the contract. If they do bring your idea to market but fail to sell the specified minimum quantity, you still get paid the royalty on that minimum-quantity amount.

Here's how I like to structure my minimum guarantees: I start out low the first year, increase it a little the second year, and hit them between the eyes the last year. Let's say that, back when I was asking for sales projections, the sales manager said, "We can easily sell $10 million worth the first year." I might say, "You said you could sell $10 million the first year, but if you can sell $2 million, that's good enough for me."

On a 5 percent royalty, my first-year minimum guarantee payment on net sales of $2 million would be $100,000. If first-year sales exceeded $10 million, I would receive more than $100,000, but if they were less than $10 million, I would still receive $100,000. The second-year minimum guarantee might be $150,000 (4% of $3 million), the third year

$250,000 (5% of $5 million), the fourth year $350,000 (5% of $7 million), and the fifth year $500,000 (5% of $10 million).

When you structure your minimum guarantees this way, it puts the risk on the back end and gives the licensee more time to reach their own sales projections. It keeps them focused on the minimum guarantees for those first couple of years rather than on the royalty amount. It also gives them a strong incentive to get your idea to market and to put some muscle into marketing and selling it.

Many people think advances and royalties are the most important things. They're not, and minimum guarantees are—both to you and the manufacturer. Without minimum guarantees, the manufacturer could sit on your idea and delay bringing it to market or never do it. Minimum guarantees lock in the deal much tighter, and they guarantee your idea will be brought to market or that you will be paid the minimum amount and get your rights back if it is not.

If the company will not agree to a minimum guarantee, you can sometimes negotiate for an "inside/outside date" instead. This provision states that the company agrees to bring your idea to market no sooner than a specified date and no later than a specified date, and if the company fails to comply with that provision, all rights revert to you. Although this is better than nothing, it is far from ideal. Without minimum guarantees, the company can retain licensing rights to your idea even if they sell only one of your products within that time frame. So I don't recommend this option until and unless you've exhausted all other potential licensees *and* tried but failed to include minimum guarantees in your contract.

Improvements

This is extremely important, but it can sometimes be a prickly point. So I usually slide it in a little later in the negotiations process, after the manufacturer and I have reached agreement on the other major terms of the licensing deal. I always ask for ownership of any improvements that are made to my idea. The licensee "rents" the exclusive right to manufacture and market my idea, and if that involves them making improvements to my idea, that's fine with me. But they have to pay for the patents, and the patents are all in my name. I own my idea lock, stock, and barrel.

This "improvements clause" came in handy a few years back after I had negotiated and signed a licensing contract with a large label manufacturer. For about a year, I worked with a gentleman there who I thought was my ally and was trying to bring my rotating label idea to market. What he was really doing was trying to get around my patents; he actually filed a couple of patents on top of my technology. But he didn't read the fine print in the licensing contract: the clause stating I owned all improvements. The contract gave his company the right to manufacture and market my Spinformation label with his improvements—but only if they hit their minimum guarantees.

Audits

The last thing you'll want to request is the right to audit the licensee's accounting records if you suspect you are not getting paid everything you're supposed to. Auditing a company's books does not foster trust, and licensees do not like this.

So how do you get an audit clause into your contract? Well, like every other aspect of negotiating a deal, you make it fair to both you and the licensee. Here is how you do that: you ask for the right to audit the licensee if you suspect a discrepancy between how much of your product is being manufactured and sold and the royalty checks you are receiving. Then—and this is where the fair part comes in and why the company will likely agree to this clause—you agree to pay for the certified public accountant (CPA) if no significant discrepancy is found. If the CPA finds a serious error that resulted in a loss of, say, 5 percent or more in paid-out royalties, then the licensee will have to pay for the CPA's audit.

Put It in Writing

It's important to have a good paper trail of the entire contract-negotiations process. I keep copies of every piece of correspondence exchanged between a potential licensee and me. During every phone conversation and one-on-one meeting (which are rare), I take good notes, and then I send a follow-up e-mail that sums up what was said and agreed upon.

Then once a potential licensee and I agree on the big picture, I create a one-page "term sheet," also called a "licensing proposal," and send it off to the manufacturer. This says to the company, "I think we can work together, and here are the terms we have talked about." Sometimes, the manufacturer and I will have a few more conversations about the terms, and the proposal will go back and forth a couple of times, with items being crossed off, changed, or added.

Working out the main terms of the licensing agreement with the manufacturer and putting it in writing will save you a significant amount of money on attorney fees and improve your chances of closing a deal. It says to a potential licensee, "I think we can work together." The licensing proposal can then serve as the basis for creating the actual licensing contract.

That's when it's time to get the attorneys involved. Drawing up a licensing contract is expensive, and many companies have a standard licensing agreement. Let the company pay for the contract, and then have your attorney review and redline it.

How an Industrial Designer Licensed His Own Idea

Dario Antonioni, the founder and executive creative director of the hugely successful industrial design lab, Orange22, calls himself "a maker of things." For more than 10 years, Dario and his team at Orange22 have designed a wide array of innovative products for a star-studded client list that includes Aveda, Billabong, Ducati, Ralph Lauren, Sharper Image, Sony, and many others. But a few years ago, it occurred to Dario that the products he designs for his clients aren't actually "his." Although his firm has won awards for its designs and gets paid well for them, it is a onetime payment. Dario does not get a percentage of the millions of dollars' worth of sales that these products generate. At the end of the day, he is still working for someone else.

continued

Then Dario came up with a fantastic "object retention" technology that could be used in a wide variety of "organization solutions for today's digital lifestyle"—from backpacks to laptop cases, iPad cases, luggage, totes, and much more. Although he understood the basic concepts of licensing, Dario didn't really know all the ins and outs of a licensing contract—one that included all the important terms, like exclusives, royalties, minimum guarantees, and an improvements clause. But with our inventRight program, he quickly learned the right way to license his idea and cut a great deal.

Dario then negotiated a lucrative licensing contract with Cocoon International, and the company is now producing more than 200 products using his patent-pending Grid-It! technology.

Even an experienced professional product designer like Dario needs to know how to cut a good deal, to be prepared for the give-and-take that it usually involves, and to be in control of the contract-negotiation process. You should, too. Chances are, the draft contract will be lobbed back and forth and amended at least a few times. Rarely do you get everything you want, but then, neither does the licensee. With a good licensing contract, both sides feel a little pain but end up with what they need and want the most. Don't fight all the issues at one time; make a couple of changes during one go-around and a couple more the next. Just keep moving the ball down the court, and before you know it, you and your licensee will be signing on the dotted line.

Living the Dream

WHEN PEOPLE find out what I do for a living, they often wonder how successful I really am at licensing ideas to companies. They have a hard time wrapping their head around why a large corporation would want to rent an idea from someone like me—a lone entrepreneur working out of a small office in Turlock, California, with only an office manager. They question how I could possibly come up with an idea that a large company's own product development and R&D people could not. They can't imagine why a big company would even open its doors to a small fry like me.

When they find out how successful I've been at this game—that I've been able to cut great deals with dozens of corporations on more than 20 of my ideas, that the royalties have enabled me and my family to live the life of our dreams, debt free and very comfortably—they want to know how they can get companies to license their ideas, too.

"Just come up with a good idea and do the right things to get the right company to license it," I tell them. Then I give them a quick rundown of how to do that, the steps we've covered so far in this book, like studying the market, validating and protecting your idea, pitching your benefit statement and sell sheet to potential licensees, and cutting a great deal.

"That's it?" they ask. "Sounds simple."

"It is simple," I'll say. "But there's one more step to creating the licensing lifestyle. This is a numbers game. So you have to keep the ideas—and the royalties—coming."

Now I'm going to tell you how to do just that.

A Marriage Made in Heaven?

In a perfect world, every deal you cut with a potential licensee would result in a win-win licensing agreement that never needs to be amended. The licensee would quickly and adeptly bring your idea to market. They would pay all your minimum guarantees and all royalties to which you are entitled, in full and on time, for the length of the contract. Sometimes it happens that way. It is just as likely that you will need to keep your hand in the game, or at least your eye on it, to ensure that your licensee doesn't sit on your idea, try to design around your idea, or neglect to pay every dollar due to you.

The least likely of these scenarios to happen is for a licensee to design around your idea to avoid paying you royalties. As I've said before, most companies need and want ideas from entrepreneurs like you and me to compete in today's innovation-driven global marketplace. Trying to intentionally rip off independent product developers is not in their best interests. If you negotiated for an improvements clause in your licensing contract, they wouldn't get away with it, anyway—if, that is, you knew about it. That's why you need to police your licenses, as I will explain in this chapter.

The most likely of these scenarios to happen is that the licensing contract will need to be amended. During the processes of developing a product, figuring out how to package, manufacture, sell, and distribute a product, any number of circumstances can arise that require a change or addition to the licensing agreement. So you'll need to be flexible, but you also need to be smart. If you maintain a good working partnership with the company after the honeymoon, you won't be blindsided when the licensee wants to amend the contract. You'll also be in a better position to ensure that the amendment is really necessary and works for you as well as the company.

If the company has a legitimate reason for wanting to reduce the minimum guarantees, maybe you can agree to that in exchange for them limiting their exclusive to one country or to a certain product category.

As for the odds of a company licensing but never manufacturing and marketing your idea, that risk is greatly reduced by writing minimum guarantees into your contract. Because the licensee has to pay the minimum guarantees whether or not they hit their sales projections and because they can lose their licensing rights if they do not pay your minimum guarantees, it behooves them to get your product to market. But it sometimes takes a while to do that. Sometimes glitches—in the design, patenting, manufacturing, packaging, or distribution—delay the process. And sometimes markets change during the process. So you need to stay on top of the process and help in whatever ways you can after the honeymoon is over.

Then there's the matter of money, and money matters a lot. You need and deserve to be paid, and your licensee is legally obligated to meet the advance, royalty, and minimum-guarantee terms of your contract. They're also legally obligated to pay for your patents, if that clause is written into your contract as well. Rarely does a licensee delay or withhold monies they owe to a licensor or for patents. When it does happen, it is usually due to an oversight or a mistake that can be resolved by contacting the company and discussing it with them. Sometimes, though, the licensee does not have the resources to pay up, and once in a blue moon, you'll run across a company that is deliberately trying to stiff you. Whatever the case may be, you need to police your licenses so that you'll know about any discrepancies and can take appropriate action to resolve them.

A licensing partnership is a lot like a marriage. It only works when both parties are working toward a common goal. If it's a good marriage, there is an understanding of and respect for one another's needs and wants. There is a willingness to resolve differences and problems, and there is a spirit of give and take.

If it's a bad marriage—well, the sooner you recognize that, the better. Then the only good resolution is usually to end it . . . as fairly and peacefully as possible. Sometimes that means going to court and letting a judge or jury decide. Often, though, if a licensee fails to bring your idea to market within a reasonable period of time or to make your minimum guarantees and royalty payments, you can just cancel the licensing agreement.

After the Honeymoon

Contrary to popular belief, your responsibility for the success of your idea doesn't end after you've signed a licensing contract. There are still myriad reasons why your idea might not make it to market, and there are many things that can go wrong once it does. No one will be a more passionate advocate for your idea than you are, and you no doubt have some design, manufacturing, or marketing expertise to offer, too. If you're working in partnership with the licensee, the likelihood of your idea making it to market is much higher. Staying involved with the company also puts you in a better position to work with the company to amend the licensing contract if things change or don't work out as planned.

Now, some people (especially those who think of themselves as inventors) want to license their idea and have nothing more to do with bringing their product to market. Others want to control, or at least have a say in, every aspect of it—from how the product is designed to how it's manufactured, packaged, marketed, and sold. Likewise, some companies will want you to go away and never contact them again, while others will be receptive to and appreciative of your advice and assistance.

In my mind, there is no question as to whether you should be involved. It's simply a question of determining the appropriate nature and level of your involvement. And that depends, to a large extent, on the company you're dealing with and on the relationship you've built with them. That's one of the reasons I like to negotiate my own licensing terms: it helps me better understand how the company operates and to strengthen my relationship with the product manager or some other key person within the company.

During the negotiation process—and before that, when I'm trying to get my foot in the door, showing a potential licensee my idea and discussing it with them—I ask a lot of questions, do a lot of listening, and take good notes. By the time we've signed a licensing contract, I usually have an idea of how I might support the licensee in bringing my idea to market. So I offer a specific type of assistance, or I simply ask the product manager, "How can I support you in this?" At the end of the day, I want my idea to see the light of day. So I try to offer the licensee whatever assistance I can to make that happen.

You can ask for a fee for your services, and sometimes you can write your role into the contract. But I volunteer my assistance free of charge, and I usually wait until the contract has been signed to broach the topic. Sometimes they take me up on my offer and sometimes they don't.

If the company does not want me involved, I don't press it. However, I might offer my help later if I see them struggling with something. When Disney was launching a new beverage called Twist 'n' Chill that featured my rotating label technology, I sat in on some of the product development meetings, and I could see they were having trouble coming up with creative content for the label. So after one of the meetings, I quietly asked the project manager if I could help with that. Sure enough, he took me up on my offer, and I was able to help move things along.

One way to stay involved with your idea is to add some "brand standards" language to your licensing agreement. For example, you could negotiate to have final approval of all products derived from your idea as well as final approval on packaging—or try to. Most companies will not agree to this. When my partner and I (at HotPicks, my one foray into manufacturing) licensed intellectual property from Disney, the contract included many stipulations on how we could represent their brand. It also included a clause stating that Disney had to give final approval of all products before they went into production. You may be able to negotiate with your licensee for similar stipulations—but it's a long shot.

Most of the time, it's better to just offer to help if and however they need it. You can help your licensee in many ways. You can give design assistance or manufacturing advice. You can refer them to a materials vendor or a packager. You can offer to participate in any promotional activities the licensee has planned or to send a press release to your mailing list. Often, I will offer to try to get the media to write a story about the product and me, as the product's developer. You can even open a promotional door for them, as I did when I got Accudial, which licenses my Spinformation label, on "The Doctors" television show. In that case, I was totally behind the scenes; I got the ball rolling and then turned it over to Accudial's PR people.

The important thing to remember is that when you license your idea to a company, it's their baby now. Yes, you still "own" the intellectual property, but they own the product—and they're in charge of getting it to market. So you probably won't have much say, if any, in the product's name, packaging, and final design nor in how it's manufactured and sold. If you want complete control of every aspect of your idea, then licensing is not the game for you. I know it's hard to relinquish control of your creation. I had a hard time with it at first too. But I became used to it and soon came to love creating and selling my ideas, even if a company changes my idea in a way I'm not completely comfortable with. My kids used to ask, "Dad, why isn't your name on the product?" I would tell them, "The only place my name needs to be is on my check."

So if the company wants you to be involved, great! Do what you can, but take a supportive role. Be careful not to overstep your boundaries, never act as a rogue player, and always give credit to the project manager or whomever you are working with. When the company sees that you're a team player and that they can count on you, they will appreciate your contribution and work even harder to make sure your idea is a success.

If the licensee doesn't want you to be involved, step back and let them do their job. Check in once in a while, and offer your assistance again if you really feel they need it and you're confident you can help.

But don't be a pest. Respect their authority. And focus on collecting your royalty checks and creating new ideas.

Policing Your Licenses

Among the most common questions I hear from people new to licensing their ideas are, "How do I know how much of my product the licensee is really selling?" and "How do I make sure they pay me what they promised to?" There are some simple ways to police your licenses to make sure you receive all the royalties to which you are entitled.

One way is to include an audit clause in your licensing contract, which I told you about in Chapter 18, and then send in an auditor to audit the company's books if—and only if—you suspect they're selling more of your product than they're paying you royalties for. This is actually not a simple way to police your licenses. It's risky, and it's expensive. An audit is a major imposition to the licensee; it takes up a lot of their time, especially if it's a large corporation, and no company likes someone going through all their accounting records. If no serious discrepancy is found, you'll have to pay the cost of the audit, which can be quite expensive. However the audit turns out, it could also put a serious strain on your relationship with your licensee. So I strongly suggest you audit a licensee's books only if you have some kind of evidence indicating a discrepancy between what's being sold and what you're being paid, and only as a last resort. And be prepared to lose money if you are wrong.

There is another way to police a deal that is much simpler and won't cost you a dime: keep your eyes and ears open. Pay attention to what your licensee is doing in the marketplace. Do they have any new products? Are they selling in new product categories or new territories or new stores? Which of their products are selling well? How is your product selling? Browse the company's website, read trade magazines, go shopping, search the Internet, and talk to industry experts. Talk to the company's sales reps, and don't be afraid to ask them which products are selling well and how your product is selling. Salespeople love to talk about these things!

If while scanning the market you discover something you think is awry, call your licensee and calmly try to get to the bottom of it. Do not accuse them of wrongdoing; instead, tell them what you discovered and ask them what's going on. Maybe you found your product in a Walmart in New Jersey, and to the best of your knowledge, you've been receiving royalties only on convenience store sales west of the Mississippi. Or maybe you found that the licensee is using your idea in a new product that you were unaware of and are pretty sure you aren't receiving royalties for.

Most of the time, it's either a fumble or a dropped ball, an unintentional screwup. And it can usually be resolved or explained with a phone call to your licensee. In those rare instances when a little foul play is going on, once the company realizes you're paying attention and expecting them to pay up, they'll usually be quick to correct course and unlikely to repeat their "error." If the problem is bigger and nastier than that, you'll need to get your attorney involved.

Several years ago, I licensed my Michael Jordan indoor basketball game to Ohio Art. I was very happy with the good job they were doing keeping the Michael Jordan Wall Ball in Walmart, Toys "R" Us, and other stores around the country for years. A few years into the licensing contract, I was strolling down the cereal aisle at my local grocery store looking for clever ideas on the backs of cereal boxes, and I saw a mini-version of the Michael Jordan Wall Ball on a box of Wheaties. The first thing I thought was, *Wow! What a great job Ohio Art is doing marketing my idea.* The next thing I thought was, *Why am I not getting a royalty check for this mini-version of my idea? The company mentioned nothing about this to me!*

After I finished freaking out, I called my contact at Ohio Art and politely asked why I wasn't getting royalty checks for the mini-version of my idea. The guy stumbled a little, "Ah, well, we must have overlooked that. I'll talk to accounting and make sure you get a check for that." That's all it took to resolve the problem: a two-minute phone conversation. I didn't need to yell. I didn't need to threaten an audit. I didn't need to file a lawsuit. I just had to call, and the royalty checks for the mini-version of my idea started coming. I never even found out if they did it on purpose.

The thing is, some companies are so large that one hand doesn't know what the other arm is doing. Occasionally, someone will get lazy or try to pull a fast one. So you have to police your deals to make sure you know what the licensee is doing with your idea and that you're getting paid for it.

It's also a good idea to survey the marketplace to determine whether a potential licensee that's sitting on your idea, or one that passed on

MY ONE AND ONLY COURT BATTLE WITH A LARGE CORPORATION

So many people are afraid of having their ideas ripped off, and patent attorneys feed on that fear. I don't like using the terms rip off and steal. A better word might be infringement, and most of the time it is unintentional. I have submitted thousands of ideas over the last 30 years, and I have had only one real problem. I now believe it could have been avoided.

I had a master license for my Spinformation label technology with CCL Label. They sublicensed it to a company called Kenilworth in Ireland. Lego, a privately held company headquartered in Denmark, contacted Kenilworth asking for samples and a quote to use this label on a new toy called Bionicles. After we signed nondisclosure agreements and my office made samples, Kenilworth gave the quote and samples to Lego. Then all communication stopped.

About 12 months after our conversations ended, I returned from a six-month travel around the United States with my wife and three kids. My son's birthday was approaching and he loved Lego, so my wife purchased the new Bionicles product for him. I remember this like it was yesterday. I was out in the garage, and Janice came out with this toy in her hand and a strange look on her face. She said, "Steve, you won't believe this, but the new Lego that I bought our son has a spin label on it." My heart sunk to my feet. The first thing I did was call my attorneys.

At the time, I had multiple patents and many patents pending in many different label formats for this technology. Apparently, Lego's

continued

engineers tried to design around my patents, not realizing I also had patents pending.

I felt violated. I took it personally, and I let my emotions take over. I ended up suing Lego in federal court in San Francisco, California. My attorneys took my case on a contingency basis, since they had written all of my patents. To litigate a patent infringement case can cost upward of $1.5 million. Most attorneys won't take on a patent litigation case unless there are at least $20 million in sales. So this is not an option for most independent product developers.

It was a long, painful process. The first day in court, I remember seeing *Stephen Key Design, LLC, et al. v. Lego Systems, Inc., et al.* and thinking, *I have arrived.* I also remember watching all the attorneys from Lego and my attorneys argue over words, over interpretations of words. Instead of using gloves, they battled with words, and the judge acted as the referee.

I signed a document limiting what I can say about the case. I cannot reveal the terms of the settlement; I can only say that we settled on terms that are confidential after three years of litigation. Lego never took a license from me, and they stopped using the rotating label.

I think it was all a misunderstanding, and if my emotions and their emotions hadn't gotten in the way, I think it never would have gone to court. We would have worked it out.

Most of the time, it comes down to miscommunication between product developers and potential licensees. Sometimes companies are designing the exact same product you are, and you are not aware of it. Sometimes they don't have knowledge of all of your patents or patents pending. That's why it's smart to stay in touch with potential licensees and maintain involvement with active licensees. It's also smart to try to resolve any problems calmly and rationally by talking with one another. Once you get emotional and get attorneys involved, no one wins.

it, has brought that idea to market without your knowledge—and without paying you. It doesn't happen often, but when it does, it can be brutal. It happened to me once.

Keep the Ideas—and Profits—Coming!

No one wins at this game by beating a dead horse, nor lose by giving up too soon. So what do you do after you've shown your idea to the top potential licensees on your list and none are interested? When do you walk away from an idea?

To be completely honest, the majority of the companies that review your ideas are going to reject them. You have to get up to bat several times before you hit a home run. But let's say you've submitted your idea to 10 companies and they all rejected it. Before submitting it to your "B list" of potential licensees, you might want to reassess your idea to determine whether you should revise and resubmit it or just let it go.

Remember in Chapter 16 when I advised you to ask a potential licensee why they had rejected your idea? Did they say it was wrong for them at that time, or for that product category, or for that industry? Was it too difficult or expensive to manufacture? Did they say the technology was too advanced or too passé? Did they give you any specifics on how you might improve the idea? Were they able to recommend another company, product category, or industry for which your idea might be a fit?

Industry experts are another good source of information for evaluating why your idea was rejected. Maybe the market has changed since you developed your idea; maybe it's in a lull. Attending trade shows, reading trade magazines, talking to industry leaders, and studying the market will help you understand the market as well the marketability of your idea.

Sometimes, you can use this information to fix your idea and then resubmit it to the same companies that rejected it or submit it to other potential licensees. Sometimes you just need to keep trying—to submit it to five companies if you've submitted it to only three, to ten if you've submitted to only five. If you've tried all the midsized companies on your list of potential licensees, try the big corporations and the small manufacturers. If the idea is solid and you believe in it, you just need to keep knocking on doors until there are no more to knock on.

Other times, when you take a step back and look at the evidence, it becomes clear that you're just spinning your wheels. It's time to move on; let go of your idea and find another one. Corporations don't expect all of their ideas to pan out, and neither should you.

Don't be one of those nutty professor types who spends years and years and thousands upon thousands of dollars "inventing" something that can't be manufactured or sold. Don't cling to an idea that isn't working and that no company wants to license. Get good at letting go, and put your talent and your time where the market is. Thousands of companies out there are willing, able, and eager to license your ideas. Keep the ideas coming, and the profits will follow. I guarantee it.

What's fantastic about this game is that anyone can play it! You don't need to quit your day job or get a degree in design, engineering, or marketing. You don't need to build fancy prototypes and file expensive patents. You don't need to dream up some revolutionary new technology. You don't need to go into debt, give up your freedom, and launch a company to manufacture and market your idea yourself.

Anyone can create and license ideas following this simple 10-step strategy:

1. **Study the Marketplace.** Go shopping, attend a trade show, talk with a guru, and consult with your mentor to find a simple idea with big market potential.
2. **Innovate for the Market.** Use your creativity to add value, novelty, and pizzazz to an existing product.
3. **Prove Your Idea.** Do your homework to validate that your idea will sell and can be manufactured at the right price points.
4. **Prototype Your Idea.** Bring your idea to life using fast, inexpensive, and effective ways to create a model or other visual representation of your idea.

5. **Create a One-Line Benefit Statement.** Articulate the greatest value that your idea offers to potential licensees and their customers in one concise and compelling sentence.

6. **Create a One-Page Sell Sheet.** Show potential licensees the benefits of your idea and a visual representation of your idea in a powerful one-page ad.

7. **Protect Your Idea.** Protect your intellectual property for only $110 with a provisional patent application.

8. **Get a Company to Say Yes.** Get your foot in the door and your idea in front of potential licensees by mastering the art of cold-calling.

9. **Cut a Great Licensing Deal.** Use the right information and the right attitude to negotiate a win-win licensing agreement with a potential licensee.

10. **Keep the Ideas and Profits Coming!** Work in partnership with your licensees, police your licenses, and move on to the next idea. Keep innovating, and keep selling your ideas.

All you need to create the life of your dreams are these 10 simple steps for bringing ideas to market—and one simple idea. Then another simple idea. And another simple idea . . . You get the idea.

Appendix

Valuable Resources

For Web links, addresses, phone numbers, and additional information for the following resources and many other resources, visit http://www.stephenkey.com/resources.

- **Books on patents.** There are dozens of books on patents, some much more useful than others. On our Resources page, you will find the patent books I recommend, including some great references books on patents written by David Pressman, a patent attorney.
- **Business and motivational books.** Over the years, I've read quite a few good books that might help you out. For a list of business and motivational books I recommend—including my all-time favorite, *The Magic of Thinking Big*—visit our Resources page.
- **Company phone numbers.** We've found WhitePages.com to be the most useful and accurate tool for looking up the phone numbers of potential licensees (and other companies) in the United States. You'll find a link to WhitePages.com and several other websites, as well as search techniques you can use to find company phone numbers, on our Resources page.
- **Contact names.** Getting your foot in the door of a potential licensee or getting advice about something along the way will be much easier if you have the name of someone to contact.

LinkedIn.com and Jigsaw.com are great websites to look up and communicate with specific contacts at companies. You can search both sites by company name and job title.

- **Engineering associations.** When you're developing your idea and need expert advice on a certain aspect of its design, these trade associations are a great place to find creative people with technical expertise. Several engineering associations are listed on our Resource page.

- **Entrepreneur websites.** There are many websites that are useful to product developers and entrepreneurs. On our Resources page, we maintain a list of these sites, which is always changing and growing.

- **Foreign patent offices.** Most industrialized countries have a patent office. For a complete list of patent offices around the world, visit our Resources page.

- **Free business counseling.** The Small Business Administration (SBA) is a great place to get free general business advice. In our experience, they don't have licensing experts to consult with; however, they do provide some great advice in other areas of business. Visit our Resources page to get the latest link to their small business planner website as well as the phone number to their answer desk.

    SCORE (Society Core of Retired Executives) is another organization that offers free business counseling. Former retired executives volunteer their time to offer business advice.

    If you are clear on what kind of help you are looking for, both organizations can help; if you're not clear, you probably won't get much out of these organizations. Some of the SBA and SCORE counselors can be very helpful, but you will need to ask for the specific type of help you are looking for to get to the right person. Otherwise, you'll just get a brochure and the canned advice everyone else gets.

- **Government programs for inventors.** The National Technology Transfer Center links U.S. businesses with federal labs and universities that have the technologies, facilities, and researchers that they need to maximize product development opportunities. The

U.S. Department of Energy Efficiency and Renewable Energy (EERE) invests in clean-energy technologies that strengthen the economy, protect the environment, and reduce dependence on foreign oil. Get the latest links from our Resource Page.

- **Graphic designers and video makers.** As you know from reading this book, quite often you don't need to make a prototype. Many ideas can be licensed using a one-page sell sheet or a sell-sheet video—both of which are an economical and effective alternative to an expensive looks-like/works-like prototype. For a list of several vendors who can make or help you make your sell sheets and sell-sheet videos, visit our Resources page.
- **Industrial design associations and schools.** If you are a product scout, these associations and schools are great places to find creative people with ideas and product design skills. We list several on our Resources page.
- **Intellectual property.** Patents, copyrights, trademarks, and trade secrets are all considered intellectual property. From the U.S. Patent and Trademark Office (USPTO) website to the Library of Congress website, get the critical links you need to learn more about and to protect your intellectual property on our Resources page.
- **Invention contests.** If you want to submit your idea to a contest, our Resources page includes links to invention contests for adults as well as a few for kids. Please note that invention contests are something fun to do on the side, but you should never use contests as your sole means of licensing ideas—and you should limit what you say about your idea publicly.
- **Invention fraud.** Be very careful about doing business with companies that ask for large upfront fees to license your invention. Make sure to also check out anyone you are thinking about doing business with. For a complete list of resources and advice, visit our Resources page, where you'll find links to patent offices, the U.S. Federal Trade Commission, and others.
- **Inventors' associations.** For a comprehensive list of inventors associations, groups, and clubs around the United States and abroad, visit our Resources page. These are great resources for educa-

tional purposes, for getting help with your ideas, and for connecting with other independent product developers.

- **Major retailers.** One of the best ways to find potential licensees is to go shopping. The companies whose products are already on store shelves at your local retailer or already being sold through catalogs and online shopping sites are often candidates for many ideas. For an up-to-date list of major retailers and how to find them, simply visit our Resources page.
- **Manufacturing directories.** If you need to research how to manufacture your idea or to get quotes on the cost of manufacturing your idea (both of which I recommend you do before you start submitting your idea to potential licensees), we have a list of free manufacturing directories on our Resources page that will help you out tremendously.
- **Patent attorneys.** The USPTO's website lists every patent attorney and agent licensed to practice in the United States. For the current link to this list, visit our Resources page.
- **Patent research.** For most people, downloading individual patents using Google Patents to research "prior art" will be sufficient. Our Resources page gives you the link to Google Patents, which you can use to download patents completely free.

  However, if you are doing some serious patent research and need to download several patents, you might consider using patent downloading software. On our Resources page, we've got a list of both Mac and PC software you can purchase to manage this process for you.
- **Prototypes.** People who make prototypes go by a few different names, including model maker, industrial designer, rapid prototyping specialist, 3-D print maker, CAD designer, machinist, and computer animator ("virtual" prototypes). Which one is right for you depends on the type of prototype you need (if you need one at all). For more information on what each type of prototyping specialist does and on how to find people with these skills, visit our Resources page.
- **Provisional patent application software.** Yes, there is actually a computer program that walks you through the process of filing your own provisional patent application (PPA). I personally use

such software and have found that it really helps speed up the process of filing a PPA. Visit our Resources page to learn more about your options for filing a PPA using software.

- **Setting up your business.** A company name, business structure, dedicated phone number, and e-mail are all important things to think about. Visit our Resources page to find out where and how to get what you need.

- **Shopping search engines.** Shopping search engines are a great way to do research. They are a little different than regular search engines in that the search results are based on products available for sale on the Internet. You should use a shopping search engine every time you come up with a new idea. It is easy and will likely provide some valuable information. Google Product Search is one of our favorites; get the link by visiting our Resources page.

- **Trade show directories.** You'll find links to three killer trade-show directories on our Resources page. These directories are certain to include at least one trade show for a product, product category, or industry that fits with your idea.

- **U.S. Patent and Trademark Office.** The USPTO is the governing agency responsible for establishing patent law in the United States and issues all patents in this country. The agency has many people ready to assist you; they even have an Inventors Help line to answer your questions. On our Resources page, you'll find all the direct links and phone numbers to the most important resources the USPTO has to offer—from fee schedules to patent searching, and beyond.

Index

About the Author

STEPHEN KEY has been a successful entrepreneur and award-winning product developer of more than 30 years. He has licensed more than 20 of his ideas and holds 13 patents. His products have been sold in major retailers throughout the world and have been endorsed by basketball great Michael Jordan and "Jeopardy" host Alex Trebek.

Stephen's innovative Spinformation® rotating label (www.spin-labels.com) has been licensed for use on many products, including Accudial®. Together with his partner, Andrew Krauss (President of Inventor's Alliance), the two have been educating entrepreneurs and inventors for the past ten years.

Recognized as an outstanding leader in the field of innovation, Stephen has appeared on national television numerous times, including an appearance on the CNBC show "The Big Idea with Donny Deutsch" and as an expert guest on "Dr. Phil." He was also a consultant on the first season of the hit ABC reality TV show "American Inventor," created by Simon Cowell. Stephen has been interviewed by national magazines, newspapers, and authors such as Tim Ferris (The 4-Hour Work Week) and Donny Deutsch (The Big Idea). Stephen is also the licensing and inventing expert at AllBusiness.com (A Dunn & Bradstreet Company), and was a keynote speaker at the United States Patent & Trademark Office 14th Annual Independent Inventor Conference in November 2009.

Stephen shares a home in Modesto, California, with his beautiful wife, Janice. The Keys have three children, two of whom attend Berkeley and one of whom attends the University of Oregon—thanks to their dad's success in licensing ideas.